Bye-Bye, Budapest

Bye-Bye, Budapest

An Autobiography

Agnes Kabdebo-Gedeon

Copyright © 2011 Agnes Kabdebo-Gedeon

The moral right of the author has been asserted.

Apart from any fair dealing for the purposes of research or private study, or criticism or review, as permitted under the Copyright, Designs and Patents Act 1988, this publication may only be reproduced, stored or transmitted, in any form or by any means, with the prior permission in writing of the publishers, or in the case of reprographic reproduction in accordance with the terms of licences issued by the Copyright Licensing Agency. Enquiries concerning reproduction outside those terms should be sent to the publishers.

Matador
5 Weir Road
Kibworth Beauchamp
Leicester LE8 0LQ, UK
Tel: (+44) 116 279 2299
Fax: (+44) 116 279 2277
Email: books@troubador.co.uk
Web: www.troubador.co.uk/matador

ISBN 978 1848766 143

British Library Cataloguing in Publication Data.
A catalogue record for this book is available from the British Library.

Typeset in 11pt Garamond by Troubador Publishing Ltd, Leicester, UK

Matador is an imprint of Troubador Publishing Ltd

Dedication

To my parents, Lily and Laszlo Wohl, who brought me up with much love,
and prepared me for life.

And to my grandsons, Toby and Robin, to help them understand their Granny,
and the story of her life.

Acknowledgements

This book could not have been written without the help and encouragement of a number of contributors and friends. My thanks go firstly to my daughters, Lily and Andrea, whose contributions help to complete this picture of their mother, to our writing group, The Thursday Group: Betty Gallimore, Pat Mastropietro, Elizabeth Parish and Rosemarie Sumira, who listened week after week to my renderings, and were a sounding board whose comments and criticisms were always sympathetic and constructive, and to Elizabeth Parish, my long-suffering editor, whose painstaking corrections have rendered my text into an English without too much of my 'charming accent.' Her constant help, guidance and encouragement has been invaluable.

Contents

Prologue	xi
Budapest Sparkle: First Impressions	xiii
A Second Glance	xvi
Early Days	**1**
Where I Was Born	3
Me at 5	10
First Days at School	14
War Years	18
After the War	25
Life Before the Revolution	38
A Little Dagger and a Big Bottle	49
Crossings	**51**
I am a Refugee	53
Channel Crossing	58
New Beginnings	61
Surprise Visit	70
Married	74
Life in London	79
Three Years in Guyana	**89**
London to Georgetown	91
Mosquitoes	98
Our Houses	99
Life in Guyana	107
Shopping	117
The Interior and its People	121
Crossing the Essequibo	127
A Trip to Sao Paulo	134
Caribbean Travels	138
Parking the Pets	145

I Remember- *Lily's Memories*	147
Sailing Home	151

Back to London — 155
A Short Detour	157
Life Day by Day	163
Why Manchester?	169

The Next Move — **173**
Meet Manchester	175
Two Houses	176
Gathering Clouds	181
Tam Leaves	187
Camper Van Arrives	191
Austrian Christmas	198
Round Trip to Bilbao	203
Animal Sacrifice	209

After Arzen — **215**
Without Arzen - Laurel Court	217
Shopping	219
Easter	220
Resentment	221
If It Was Death	223
Funeral	226
Maroon Balloons	228

Epilogue — **231**
Life Goes On	233

Prologue

Budapest Sparkle
Memories of Lily Kabdebo

First Impressions

Not all that long ago, on 6*th* March 1936, somewhere in Budapest a baby girl was born to Laszlo and Lily Wohl. My mother explained that she was a child diagnosed by doctors as having an unusually large heart which her body then grew to accommodate.

As she described it, my mother's childhood appeared to have been tattooed by the terror of foreign troops occupying Budapest during the Second World war. In my own childhood, she described more than once the fear of lying in bed at night on the first floor of the typical Budapest quadrangled tenement block where she lived with her parents. The sound of heavy footsteps in the balcony corridor lining the courtyard on each storey had often scared her. They might have been soldiers coming for her father.

My grandfather had been a hatter – with his own business. This kind of entrepreneurship was frowned upon during communist times and had eventually been sufficient to bar her entry to university, although she had the grades.

I heard about the twins – her close girlfriends who lived nearby and later both emigrated to America. She never lost contact with them until one died a few years ago.

One summer, when I was twelve or thirteen, while standing, leaning against the strong, but spindly and precarious looking iron railings of the corridor of that same tenement balcony, waiting for my grandmother to appear, I peered down into the courtyard. I wondered aloud to my mother and little sister what it must be like to fall from there. My mother then recounted the story of a girl in a block nearby, a teenager around the same age as I was then, who had actually met her end in this way after the war years – a troubled soul apparently, who had flung herself off on purpose; I don't recall exactly what my mother said had moved her to do this – some family troubles heightened by the war, or her love life, perhaps?

My mother often told me stories about her diminutive yet engaging cousin Tomi, who also lived nearby. My mother adored Tomi. He treated her like a grown up – taking her dancing, entertaining her with jokes and giving her, I think, bags of confidence in life. They were very close, and his mother was my mother's confidante. While her relationship with her own mother was thorny, this aunt (affectionately named 'Little Blessing') would always soothe her path.

My mother was naughty sometimes – not always sticking to the time she'd tell her mother she'd be home after a day on the river Danube (she is a keen rower). She could wind up her mother in classic teenage daughter style, and my grandmother would be harsh in verbal retaliation. Granny was a supreme artist in taking, and then creatively sustaining an offended attitude. But Little Blessing (also tiny in stature) was always there to understand.

My mother also adored her father. He was passionate about her learning to ice skate and by the age of 14 she was of competition standard, attaining outstanding places in junior championships. She said that she went up to that level to please him, especially after he left home when she was 13. She was angry with him, but wanted to keep his love. She said that it took her a long while to accept Eva, his new wife. However, in later years, following the emigration of Tomi and his parents to Brazil. and later, the death of Little Blessing, my mother and Eva grew to have an adult appreciation of each other, which in my child's eyes, appeared close and friendly. I knew my mother could confide in her too – enough to be able to express some of the lows following her divorce from my father, and enough to value Eva's advice and words of comfort. My mother is a regular, committed and conscientious letter writer and has included Eva in her correspondence as long as I can remember. Eva also produced Lacko – my mother's half brother and possibly her best friend on mainland Europe.

Alongside bombs and footsteps in the passageway, also featuring largely in my mother's childhood were water and music. Her father provided her with a taste for riverside nature, cultivating a common Budapester's love of excursions from the capital to the surrounding countryside.

Her mother encouraged her to play the piano – to the extent, my mother told me, that she had ambitions to be a concert pianist - but she later swapped these dreams for architecture, since she was apprehensive for her future if she did not make it into the top ranks of performance. Luckily for me, though my parents lived frugally in my early years they found money to buy a piano. My father loved to hear my mother play, and it made me want to play too and to dance. In my early childhood her passion for playing the piano was strong. Night after night, I was lulled to sleep through her expressive renditions of Mozart's, Chopin's, Kodaly's, Bartok's and Beethoven's keyboard creations.

My mother often spoke fondly about her childhood piano teacher who remained a life-long friend of my grandmother. I remember meeting her at my grandmother's apartment when I was a child, and again as an adult, when living in Budapest. I asked her for advice about which notes to buy in order to practise Hungarian style.

To me, as a child, my grandmother's apartment appeared to be part of a grand old six or seven storey block - despite the fragile and rickety gas heater in the bathroom, and in later years, the large, unsanded wooden beams placed inside and outside along the walls and ceilings to hold it up. It had tall windows and even taller ceilings and old parquet floors. It overlooked a well-frequented side street on one side and a cobble-stoned, rectangular courtyard on the other. The flat was a stone's throw from Budapest's imposing Opera along one of the town's main boulevards.

Many little girls grow up with fantasies of becoming models, ballerinas and actresses. My mother's fantasy was to sing, or at least to somehow live in an opera. Despite being talented for the keyboard she lacked the confidence to sing, claiming she had a terrible voice. Consequently, she encouraged my sister and me to use ours all the more. My mother's love of opera grew and is part of her today. It was with her all through our family life – as she would arrange it regularly around radio transmissions of live performances. Thus, over many weekends, the effect of opera seeped into my sister's soul. In mine it was subconsciously stored away for indulgence later on.

A Second Glance

I had not formulated a concept of my mother's personality as a child and young teenager until one day, a few years ago, while I was visiting her brother Lacko in Hungary. he showed me a very short black and white silent cine film clip. It was of my mother ice skating on an open air rink in Budapest, followed by a summer family gathering by the Danube. I was riveted. Here was this attractively mufflered 13-year old with plaits that reached her waist, spinning and cruising so adeptly on ice.

As a child I'd always enjoyed the stories she'd tell me as often as I'd asked about the behind-the-scenes bitchy, competitive, shenanigans of the skating girls., and how they or their mothers would deliberately sabotage each other's skates in various ways to take the edge off each other's performances.

A low pirouette

Whenever my mother had taken me and my sister ice skating as children she had always moved so modestly – showing us the basics in an understated yet accomplished style. I'd only heard her talk of jumping and spinning, but now, albeit for a few monochrome seconds, I was actually seeing her spirit.

What struck me even more in the summer part of the film clip was the innocent and radiant joie de vivre emanating from my mother – a super friendly, smiling teenager with 'I want to please you and I know how' branded on all her facial expressions and gestures. And then they all made sense, my father's remarks about what a fabulously willing person my mother was – when (and why) he married her.

In winter 1956, as many were leaving Hungary, my grandfather paid for a guide to help my mother pick her way through the minefields of no-man's land to Austria. At a camp in Salzburg my mother interpreted for officials and fellow refugees, using her German and English language skills. She said that at one point she was even offered some spying work.

At the close of the sixties and beginning of the seventies, I had what I considered to be a 'real mother' – she came to pick me up from school in the car! In London, by the age of eight, I had become used to walking home alone from school, letting myself into our flat, feeding the cat, snooping about in private drawers, inventing unusual sandwiches for myself and practising the piano until our adopted English aunty-cum-childminder would bring my sister home.

In Georgetown I had more attention paid to me. For a period my mother was not able to work, and attended coffee mornings and dress-making classes instead. So she made us all clothes and encouraged me to design my own for a local dressmaker to sew. She also crotcheted and taught me how. She took my sister and me to origami classes after school and she had time to love our numerous pets.

In view of the strong city upbringing she had, I have always been impressed by how natural she was with our pets in South America, and how she continued to be so back in the UK. On the surface it was my father who had the sound knowledge and confidence in dealing with nature, since hunting, fishing and helping wounded animals was part of his survival training by his own father. His family had been forced to live in a forest near his home town in southern Hungary during the war years. My mother, however, had that playful love for our pets that passes onto children quite easily. We even kept a horse between the stilts under our house in Georgetown, and this did not appear to phase her or affect any of her city sensibilities. She even learnt to ride, and so came to accompany me in that activity also.

Following our family's stay in Guyana, back in London there were some unhappy times, as there had been while I was a child in Fulham before we left for Guyana. My father suffered a bout of depression similar to one he had experienced during my earlier childhood. At that time, he was in a mental hospital with extensive grassy grounds, and I remember visiting him after his electric shock treatment. He knew us, but had temporarily lost some of his memory for people and names. He made interesting plaster-of-paris sculptures and covered ceramic pots in tasteful mosaics in art therapy sessions there. and he began to teach me to play snooker. I remember anticipating his coming home, and my mother organising a surprise furnishing of his compact study with a lining of shelves from desk top to ceiling on every wall.

On our return from Guyana, possibly because I was older, my memories of my father's condition are more disquieting. I thought at the time I was miserable mainly from missing the pets, heat, colours, sounds and vibrancy of Guyana, but the truth was also that my father could be manic at times – suddenly pulling the tablecloth from beneath the breakfast paraphernalia just before my sister and I were about to leave for school. Sometimes he would lie in bed for hours on a Saturday morning, and I have known him to hurl a cup of cocoa across their bedroom. After this, he wrote lists of instructions to himself and my mother concerning behaviour, and then stuck these on the wall above their double bed.

As a young teenager, dragged reluctantly back to Europe from the Caribbean, I enjoyed my mother's quartz sun lamp a lot. I had grown into a true sun addict – just like her. I became fanatical about table tennis – attending an evening club at the end of our road about three times a week for training. It was possibly a kind of escape from home after my father took a job in Manchester, since for about six months we could only see him at weekends.

In the sixties, my mother made me wear some fabulous and some unbearable dresses. Meanwhile, every morning I would watch her dressing in what always appeared to be such slick outfits – especially her quality autumnal wool suits in their deep, natural, seasonal colours and her fashionable knee high silver boots.

She always had what I described as that beige Mediterranean, European skin tone – so much more welcoming to me than the brighter, white more arid faces that my English friends' mothers appeared to have. Even today, as an older citizen, despite the increased numbers and depths of character lines on her face, she has the arresting, questioning green eyes that nobody else's mother has. She has spontaneous, unexpected humour, more patience, and some wells of wisdom, freed in maturity to bubble up to the surface and express themselves . Now that she lives more alone than not, Nan, next door, is the person who mostly receives those immediate attentions towards a 'significant other'.

At home, creativity, curiosity and practicality have a freer reign in her life than they have had for *a while. Post operative recovery spurs her development in all these directions — if only she'd acknowledge the ultimate developer and source of all these gifts and accompany me to church. Today, through her own efforts and with God's help, this older lady with a larger than ordinary hole in her abdomen has already grown sufficiently to accommodate it.*

Early Days

Where I Was Born

Lazar-u is a side street in Budapest city centre. The Opera House is at one end of the street and St Stevens Basilica is at the other. In Lazar-u some aristocrat had built his town house. Later, the building had been converted into flats, and I lived in one of them.

It must have been quite easy to carve modern flats out of the old imposing reception rooms on the street side of the building. But the designers must have had a tough task to provide flats around the other three sides of an enclosed courtyard where once upon a time the servants' quarters had been. An open, hanging corridor solved the problem, and gave access on both the first and the second floors.

My earliest memories are mixed up with photos, and I don't really know if I actually remember or I visualize an old photo. Later on sounds became more reliable, they create triggers, and I can certainly remember events by them.

Lying in bed - on one of those divan beds which converted into seating during the day – I can always hear her footsteps from the street. These are the days of high heels, and I can recognise my mother's unmistakable steps, light and rapid. Soon, she will come in through the gate.

In the old days, when the gate was fully opened, carriages passed through: now, only half of it opened. Then, to the right, there was the spacious, pink coloured marble staircase. Three long flights to each floor ran around a wide stair well with handrails broad enough to be used as slides – that was: one of our favourite pastimes when no one saw us. There were several children of different ages in the building, and I joined them very young. The wrought iron balustrades were not childproof either. We cheerfully passed between them and used the projecting ends of the steps to go up and down, hanging on to the rails. We were not thought to be in any danger.

From the staircase an open corridor leads to our front door. I can hear my mother when she turns the key in the lock of the door, then she walks through the long hall to a set of fully glazed double doors, which give borrowed light to a window-less space we use as our dining room. It is furnished in sort of art deco style. There is a heavy oval table, made of mahogany and polished to perfection, with six very high backed chairs upholstered in burgundy coloured embossed velvet material. A large sideboard with rounded corners takes up a whole wall. Behind one of its curved doors there are several shallow drawers for cutlery. I have always wondered if my parents wanted to match the curve of the oval table, but I never asked. In childhood these things are taken absolutely for granted. Furniture simply belongs.

My mother walks through to another set of double doors which lead to a large room facing the street below. In summertime these double doors are kept open. Here are two large, inter-connecting rooms. Mine is the smaller of the two. Both have high ceilings and in the thick walls are windows opening to the street. The windows are wide, at least one and a half metres. There are two of them to my parents' room, and one to mine. The windows are double sashes, and open inwards. In winter, the second sash is hinged on and the shutters closed in the evenings to keep the warmth in. Heavy net or crocheted curtains reach to the floor. These are not for added insulation, simply 'window-dressing'. Stripy hangings and a pelmet finishes the picture. I didn't know then that after the war, one of these hangings would provide dress material for a special occasion.

Double doors in the flat

My mother reaches their room, next to mine. The parquet floor of intricate square patterns echoes her steps between the rugs. Some of them are real Persian; some are hand made by her. I still treasure some today in my home. They are well travelled rugs – not quite like Sinbad's flying carpet – but they were smuggled out of Hungary in an equally strange way.

My mother puts down her keys on a low, long dressing table with its three small drawers, and she has a glimpse of herself in the tall mirror above it. The unit and the mirror frame are of the same French polished mahogany. A round coffee table stands in the corner with three easy-chairs of the same wood. The legs are all carved to look twisted, and the seats and the backrests are of rattan. All fits comfortably in front of the stove, which stands diagonally in the corner. Spring was particularly cold in the year of 1936 when I was born, and even now the white-tiled wood burning stove is fully in use, even in May. Mother walks to the hot, shiny tiles to warm her hands.

In front of the two large windows stands my black baby-grand, with its matching, circular stool that can be wound up and down. When I started to play, a small toy chest was placed under my feet. It was decorated with pretty tulips painted on white background, and I often wondered if they would get damaged by my feet.

In my room, my father's large old writing desk sits by the window. I am very proud of it, and I am the envy of my contemporaries who have to do their homework on childish desks. However pretty these are, I have the real thing. It is black, and has drawers on one side and a door with shelves behind on the other.

A large four-door combination unit at the back of the room holds my worldly possessions. The middle two doors are glazed but have white net curtains on the inside. I think this section is meant for books, but it is used for all sorts of things, so they have put up the curtains to hide them. And I have a shelf unit, of course, for toys to begin with. and for books later on.

Having warmed her hands, my mother dons her slippers, and goes on her way. She takes out her keys again, which dangle and rattle on a large key ring, and she unlocks one of the wardrobe doors. The keys make a noise wherever she goes. She has this bunch of keys with her all the time, like the keeper of a castle, our home.

After breakfast she unlocks the pantry. This has a light-well, no bigger than about two metres square, which lets in some light and air. She takes out the foodstuff for the day for the maid to cook, and then she locks the pantry door.

The keys are used again to take the laundry basket out of its place. My mother goes through all the dirty linen the day before laundry day. She also teaches me

My father at his writing desk

how to do it. I have to count so many vests, knickers, socks and blouses. Her list is of course longer, it contains household linen and so on. On laundry day, when the washerwoman arrives early the laundry list is ready for her.

The wash is prepared in the kitchen, and water is boiled on all four gas rings of the cooker. I am not really allowed to be around. Steam rises and finds its way to the other rooms, although the flat was rather large. I know what will be for lunch: soup and some sort of pastry. It is a foregone conclusion. It is the custom that there is no meat when the washerwoman comes. Poor woman, I hate to think of the diet she has to manage on while doing heavy physical work. Once the washing is done she has to carry the wet, clean load up to the loft, where clothes are hung up to dry. The keys have to be obtained from the concierge, but all tenants have access to this space. Still, I don't recall that anything ever went missing.

The morning routine over, the keys stop rattling and they have a rest in their special place until my mother wants to use them again. She is always suspicious, and wants to avoid tempting the domestics to steal. I believe I have acquired my dislike of keys from her practice.

The kitchen is a long way away. I have nothing to do with it. I can recall my father picking up my mother in his arms and bringing her out of the kitchen. Happy days. My father has not much to do with the kitchen either, except when he deposits the results of a day's shooting. I am never allowed to see what goes on

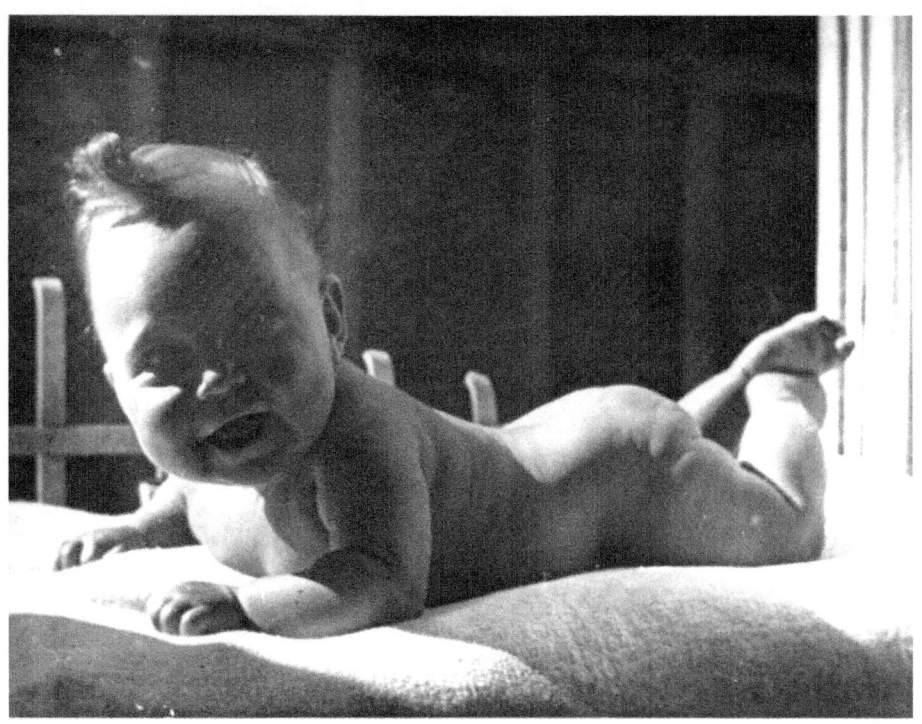

Lying on a wide window-sill

then: the cleaning, skinning and processing of pheasants, hare or deer. But I do remember these being served up on our plates.

As the seasons change and temperatures drops below 10 degrees centigrade, the winter rituals begin. Double glazing goes back on the windows. With the secondary frames off in the summer the window sills were some four inches wider and provided a very useful horizontal surface to play or to sit on.

A large white wardrobe stands in the hall and serves for seasonal storage rather than daily usage. It is now ceremoniously opened, and suddenly the smell of moth balls fills the entrance. My mother announces it is time for winter coats. Out come all the family overcoats, scarves, muffs, gloves, hats, cap - everything, including the rubber overshoes.

My mother slips into her black, shiny, low heeled over-boots. She walks very well in them, although her ordinary shoes are on her feet too. These galoshes are excellent in the rain, but, surprisingly, people wear them even in snow. How they don't slip and break their limbs, I will never know. The equivalent of today's apres ski 'moon boots' are aired too. As a child I do not qualify for the elegant shiny

Snow piled high on a Budapest street

black overshoes, but I do have miniature moon boots. We know it is only a matter of days until the temperature will plummet and snow will be with us.

And so it happens. People appear with shovels to clear the pavements. They heap the snow into large mounds half on the pavement, half on the carriageway. It is fun to run or slide up and down these, instead of walking straight. Sometimes they are so high that from the path I cannot see the cars. But I am quite small, of course. Even when there are no others around I simply must make snow balls and aim at targets - practising, you understand, for the real battles to come. My gloves are soon soggy and cold, and my fingers are rigid.

Many years later, I was lucky enough to be able to show my children where I grew up, just before my mother moved away. We walked down the narrow street and I whistled the same family tune my father taught me as a child to let mother know of our arrival. She was at home, expecting us, and we stayed with her in the same old rooms.

When I next visited the place with my young niece who was being introduced for the first time to the country of her ancestors, tall hoardings lined the street where my home used to be. In between the panels we could see the cellars of the old building. A ramp led from the street and youngsters were happily skateboarding on the slope. The place I was born to and left after twenty years had been demolished.

My Mother, Grandmother, and Kis Kereszt

On holiday with cousin Tomi and his family

Me at Five

I was an only child, and I think I lacked company of my own age. My Granny lived with us and she played interminable games with me. She also took me to the local playground where I met other children. It was at this playground that I was bitten by a small dog, probably because I ran around too near to the bench under which it sat and watched us. Its owner was sitting on the bench and she was very apologetic, but my Granny was not too pleased. The bite stung, so Granny took me to a nearby first aid place, where they disinfected the bite, and bandaged it.

As an only child I spent too much time among grown-ups, and I became very serious. There were strict rules: always greet grown ups first; don't run around on the open corridor; always shut doors etc. etc. These didn't make much sense to me – therefore, at an early age, I learned how to get around them. This became very useful later on, when I had to survive under the changing, but equally oppressive regimes which followed one another.

I remember how I was in those days, a wide eyed child with a pale face, green eyes and rather heavy arched eyebrows.

In an oil painting of my Grandmother as a young woman, a large photo of my Mother, and a picture of me at age three the family resemblance is plain to see. My blond hair was taken back off my face into short plaits with taffeta ribbons woven through them. To achieve this was a daily ceremony performed either by my Mother or by Granny. I don't remember the clothes I had, but the colour of the ribbon usually had something to do with the colour of my dress. There was often discussion over this, for a consensus had to be reached between Mother and Granny.

First, however, they had to get me out of bed. I hated getting up, though it was fun to be half asleep, sitting up in bed with the duvet wrapped around me and my

Me at age five

feet dangling. I began dressing under the covers, though how I managed it I can no longer figure out. Mother pulled horrible ribbed stockings up to my ankles and laced my boots over them. Then I had to get up, to put on the worst thing of all, the contraption that held up those stockings. There were straps like halters to go over my shoulders on top of my vest. These were connected to a waist band. At that tender age I had no real waist. Attached to the band were suspenders which actually gripped the stockings. I hated the whole affair and could hardly wait for spring when I could wear socks. On really frosty days I had to put on a pair of trousers on top of the stockings. Some of these were hand knitted, probably by Granny and I liked these soft rather loose, ribbed garments. I could not understand why I was not allowed to wear them on their own, but in temperatures reaching below minus ten centigrade it was necessary to wrap children up as warmly as possible.

With a bonnet on my head, tied with a ribbon under my chin, I was taken the short distance to the posh, multi-lingual nursery school where I began to learn smatterings of German and English. Perhaps this was second sight on the part of my parents, or perhaps it was simply the accepted pattern for a well brought up youngster. I don't know. I simply looked forward to getting there and always enjoyed being there.

At the end of the morning session I was taken home by another mother, and dropped off at the wooden gate to our building. From here I was allowed to go alone up to the first floor and along the long open corridor to our apartment. By then it was nearly lunch time, but I was not usually hungry. I did not eat much at the best of times, though when food became scarce I started to ask for more. Typical, people often said.

One day we finished a bit earlier. It was not quite lunchtime, and so I walked on past our gate. At the end of our short street stood the Opera House – an Italianate building, I later learned, built by a famous architect in the previous century. On three sides it had entrances for the public, and the stage entrance was from our street. The public entrances all had gently curving drives for carriages leading to a flight of steps up to entrances with large double doors some way above street level. The carriageways were flanked by wide convex kerbs about a foot high with elaborate mouldings. They were not meant for walking on, but children did climb them, and whenever I had to walk that way I always went up and down. It was so much more fun than walking on the ordinary pavement. But usually I had only time to do it once, if I was not to be left too far behind, and there was certainly no time to climb up to the large stone Sphinx which terminated the kerb. "Now, I've got time for a few runs," I thought to myself, and the deed followed the thought. Up and down I ran, thoroughly enjoying myself. I didn't even climb the Sphinx, I just ran up and down, carefully balancing, for I didn't want to fall.

I did not notice the car which pulled up very quietly, practically next to me, but as I completed the next run down, I bumped into my mother.

She didn't say a word. Possibly she didn't know what to say. My father got out of the car in silence. For a long moment nobody said anything.

Then: "What are you doing here?" A gentle question, almost like a sigh, from my mother.

"She must know," I thought. "She saw me all right. Why ask?" But I dared not break the silence.

They bundled me into the car and we drove around the corner – less than a minute's drive – to the house. Still neither of them said a word. In complete silence they marched me between them along the long corridor to our flat. By now I was thoroughly scared. I wished they would say something. I knew very well that I should have come straight home, that I should never have made that little unaccompanied excursion. And that is just what my father said.

"Were you brought home from nursery school?" he asked.

"Yes, I was," I heard myself answering. Did I detect a smile on his face?

"What do you think her punishment should be?" He turned to my mother.

Punishment? I don't think I had ever heard the word before.

"Her bottom should certainly be smacked," was the answer.

I had never experienced such a thing. The worst that had happened before was perhaps a quick, instant slap when I had really overstepped the mark.

The smack was certainly not hard, nor particularly painful, but to suffer the indignity of lying on the big bed on my stomach to receive it, was very bad. Luckily, it was one of those cold days when I wore knitted trousers and the ribbed stockings, so there was no skirt to lift. But it was bad enough.

I had known, all the time I was enjoying myself, that I was breaking the rules, but I only learned later in life, when I had children of my own, what my parents must have felt.

First Days at School

Nursery school has been fine, but now I know all the games and the activities we do. After all, I had been there for a long time. Years and years. And most of my friends have left they are now in proper school. Proper school is even nearer to my home, so when I get there I might be allowed to come and go on my own.

Here I am, ready to go to proper school. Granny has spent extra time brushing and brushing my hair. It is long now, and it is in two plaits, with just two small ribbons at the end to hold them neatly. I have a new school bag strapped to my back and an elevenses pack. In nursery, we used to have elevenses given to us.

My school is called St Steven's Square Primary. My father went to the same school and the old Headmaster remembered him when we went to our interview. Granny takes me across the main road at the end of our street. Then we pass a few big buildings at the side of St Steven's Basilica. We enter the hallway: it is quite narrow and a bit dark. I wonder how Granny knows where to go - but she does. We walk up wide stairs, flights running along three walls, though there is no well in the middle, as in our block of flats. On either side there are walls with railings. I couldn't slide down here.

We reach a wide landing and a corridor. Above a door there is some writing. I can recognise a few capital letters, but not these. Granny comes to my rescue.

"Here we are," she says. "Class 1C. There must be a lot of you if they have to have three classes." We open the door and look inside. It is a large room with windows down one side.

"Go on." Granny gently pushes me along when I stop. There are children in there. Girls are at the front and boys at the back of the room. Mummies, Grannies and just a couple of Daddies are kissing them good bye. Granny does the same.

A lady who says she is Ilonka néni, comes along and points out hooks around the walls.

"Take your jacket off and leave it here," she tells me. "Here is your name, above the hook. You will soon learn to recognise it. Take your bag with you, and let us see where you are going to sit."

There are two rows of wooden double desks. The idea is that the small children sit at the front, and taller children sit at the back of the classroom. I am ushered to a right hand seat in the second row, on the left of the room, facing the 'cathedra', the teacher's platform. I examine my desk, and I find that the desk top lifts up to reveal a compartment. I learn eventually that we keep our books and elevenses there. Then the bag stays by the coat hook. On the top of the desk, the part which doesn't lift up there is an ink well. The glass container in it is clean and empty. This looks interesting, almost like the paint pots we used to have in nursery school. There is a long groove running along the whole top. This will be for our pencils, I think.

Ilonka néni now goes to her platform and sits down behind the table. She reads out all our names from a big book. I wonder how she knows all this. We have to stand up and say "present" as she calls our names. I find out that the twins, my friends from nursery school, are here. When Ilonka néni finds out we know each other she sits Eva next to me. This proves to be a mistake. To us, sitting together means chatting together, and this is not allowed - as we soon find out. Vera, the other twin sits a row behind us. She is the tallest of the three of us, probably because she is a quarter of an hour older than Eva. That apart, should they sit together no one would ever know which was which.

In a few days we manage to learn to sit straight with our arms folded behind our backs, until we are told to do something else. Soon Ilonka néni learns our names. She calls us by our first names. It is by my first name too, that she warns me not to chat during lessons. I don't even know I am chatting. When she has had enough of it, she tells me to go and stand in the corner of the class room, on my own. I realise I am being punished.

We also have to learn to control our feet properly, with no kicking, swinging or sticking toes out into the aisle between rows of desks. Easier said than done. My feet hang out on the right hand side. I can't help it sometimes. It is after elevenses now, and I would rather be on my way home.

"How many times do I have to tell you how you should sit?" Ilonka neni asks me. "You had better go and stand on those feet of yours for a while in the corner of the room."

Must Ilonka néni notice everything? I think at first that she is talking to a girl on the other side of the classroom. I hope we will go home soon.

Yes, the bell rings and we form a crocodile, small ones at the front and taller ones at the back, and we file out of our classroom. Class 1A goes first, then B, then us. We follow the others to the staircase, down the flights winding around the walls. While we have to wait on the stairs, for those ahead of us to be met and picked up at the gate, somebody pulls one of my plaits. Automatically I turn back and hit out. I have no idea who it is, but of course there is a commotion.

"You, there – yes," and the supervising teacher points at me. This one doesn't know my name. I am pulled out of the crocodile in no uncertain terms and I have to wait by the opposite wall until all the children are gone. I am last to leave school.

I believe I hold the record for being punished for misbehaving three times in a single day.

It got better later, and my first year at school seemed to pass very quickly. I do not remember what sort of results I had, but I do remember I could read faster than most, and I was rather bored while others were reading. I started to be big headed at a very early age.

In the second year, nobody comes with me to find the new class room, I am familiar with the school building. Irén néni, our new form teacher, sits me in the first row, probably because I am quite small. Soon we have to have some kind of injection. There is a medical room in the basement, where we go in pairs and queue. There are children crying even before we go in. They put something on our arms, which feels very cold. I am not worried and I can't see what the fuss is about. Then it is just a prick, not too bad, nothing to cry about, I think.

December approaches, and Santa Claus is celebrated on the 6th. Everybody gets a little present and a message from Santa. "Don't fight when you think teacher isn't looking," is my message. I am quite intrigued. I wonder how Santa Claus knows about it. There is a faint smile on my parents' faces when I tell them about it, but there is no follow up at all.

For the Christmas holiday we are given home work. It seems a lot. I copy and copy pages and pages of text from our book. My parents are a bit surprised, but they just say, "Get on with it." I do. My copybook is nearly full. When we go back to school Irén néni gives me a strange look, and asks, "Why did you do all this? I never asked for it." Obviously I had been chatting, not paying attention when she set out the home work. Then she gets hold of a pair of scissors and cuts out all the pages from my copy book. I am mortified.

We don't do joined up writing as yet. After my marathon homework, I can do quite nice printing, but when we do joined up writing I struggle a bit. But I am keen to do it - so much so, that once when I was ill in bed, probably with a cold, I wanted to do some writing. My Granny was at home with me and she didn't think it was a good idea to use ink in my bed. However, she went out into the kitchen to do the cooking, and I knew she would be some time. I got hold of my school bag, and started to write. Of course, the inevitable happened. There was a blotch on my duvet cover. I was scared. I had heard that ink stains come out if you soak the material in milk. I don't remember how I got hold of milk and a bowl, but I do remember I had to stay very quietly in my bed with all this, so that I wouldn't make a bigger mess. What if Granny came into my room? I was worried out of my wits. By the time my mother came home I had made the milk and bowl disappear, and only a faint stain remained. Of course, she noticed it, but she didn't seem too angry. I never learned what went on between Granny and my mother about this little affair.

Another time I missed school was when I had my tonsils out. In those days they did it without general anaesthetic. I was seated in somebody's lap and they strapped me to him. Our family doctor was in the operating theatre, therefore I felt assured. I always liked him and the stories he used to tell me about the King Frog. A very strong light above us made me very hot. Then something was sprayed down my throat and I felt frozen. Our doctor explained that this would help me not to feel the needles when they gave the injections. After that everything would be numb. I believed him, and he was right. I felt no pain and I sat calmly through the operation, thinking of all the promised treats to come.

My mother stayed the first night in the clinic with me. There were no complications, and a few days later I was at home and eating. What's more, I started to eat properly. Before the procedure I had no appetite. My mother always said that while there was plenty of food I didn't want to eat. Now, when food was beginning to be scarce I wanted it. Typical.

War Years: 1944

In March 1944, the German army moved into Hungary and assumed control.

I was eight years old, and my primary schooling was interrupted. Having caught measles I was at home with Granny. I can still see her, sitting in the living room, in one of her favourite arm chairs, knitting. She had stretched a skein over the back of a chair and I wound it into a ball. Maybe the thread had been used before, I don't know. Now a thin white thread came off the neat round ball.

"What is that going to be?" I enquired, seeing her flapping knitting needles. She knitted continental fashion: I never even imagined then that there could be another way. She tried to teach me how to use theses dangerous weapons, but I could never sit still long enough. She was knitting something square-ish, with an intricate pattern.

"This will be your new cap," she said. "It will soon be finished."

And indeed it was. I had to wear this thing, all beautifully lined and with a sort of peak sticking up at the back. It was tied with a wide, white ribbon under my chin. I didn't like it at all.

The summer passed by, and I was barely aware that a war was going on, except that my father was not at home, and occasional aeroplanes flew high above. The grown ups said that the Americans were dropping bombs, but apparently they avoided Budapest.

On the 15th October, the Nazi Arrow Cross party, the Hungarian equivalent of the Gestapo, took power, and propaganda leaflets were dropped from the air. My friends and I used to run down to the street to collect them. On this warm autumn afternoon all the interior doors were open in the flat. It was about fifteen metres from the window where we were watching the leaflets coming down to the glazed front door. I missed the handle, and went straight through the glass. Blood spurted from my arm. A neighbour who was a dentist gave first aid, and he took me in his car to the nearest hospital to have me stitched up. The first hospital refused to do it, so we drove to a clinic where he had a contact. This was the first time I had a general anaesthetic using a mask. I hated it, and I have hated it ever since. They put quite a few stitches in my arm as the cut was very near to a vein

After my arm was stitched up I could not go to school for a while, and by the time I could, the schools were closed. So I was at home with Granny, who tried, with little success, to train me to do housework. Towards the end of the war there was no domestic help available in the city, and Granny ran the household. I would have much preferred school.

One day the doorbell rang. It was in the middle of the morning, and I was still in my dressing gown helping Granny. She crossed the long hall and opened the door. A man I had seen a few weeks earlier was there again. Then, he had brought bad news from my Godmother, who was afraid to leave their home. She had sent word with him about my Uncle Tibor, who had not returned home from work. He had probably been rounded up with several of his Jewish colleagues from their office in Budapest.

The man now stood in the doorway, and he asked again for my mother. She wasn't in, but I knew where she had gone: to the Swedish consulate, in Buda, on the other side of the river, up on Castle Hill. I had been there with my mother the day before. We were hoping to obtain papers for my Godmother and for my Cousin Tomi, but the queue was so long we never got in. This morning she had left very early, hoping to reach the counter.

A letter from the Swedish Consulate would place them, whose only sin was that my uncle was Jewish, under the protection of a neutral country. Not that anything was fool proof against fascist hooligans or the brutish members of the Arrow-Cross organisation. But hundreds of Jews hoped to escape the ghetto, or being shot into the river or a long march to Auschwitz. Conversion to Christianity, whether a long time earlier, or just prior to the war, counted for nothing. Even my mother was in peril, being married to a converted Jew. Jews were also required to live in houses identified with a large yellow Star of David above the main entrance. My mother had the courage to stick white crosses all over our windows: these were the permitted signs for Christian families living in blocks of flats otherwise declared 'Jewish Houses'.

But Mother was not at home, and the man said the matter was urgent. He didn't know Budapest very well and asked Granny for directions.

Still holding my toy broom and duster, I piped up, "I know where she is," to my Granny's visible dismay.

"And could you guide me there?" asked the man immediately.

Granny was not at all happy. She was undecided, and I had a sense of impending danger. I didn't know exactly what it was all about, as I had not heard what was said in the doorway.

However, I was quickly dressed, and allowed to leave with the man. He held my hand tightly all the way down to the river, and across Adam Clarke's chain bridge. Then the sirens blared out their warning of an imminent air attack. In the autumn of 1944, allied forces were bombing Nazi occupied Hungary. The bridges over the Danube were obvious targets.

We hurried across the bridge, which remained intact behind us, though it was blown up by the retiring German army a short while later. Then we had to climb the dozens of steps to the old part of Castle Hill where the consulates were. Approaching the building I saw what I had vaguely remembered - a large crest on the shiny wooden gate and a blue flag with a yellow cross on it. People were sheltering in the archway. We didn't stop, we just pushed on among the people until we found my mother.

There was a quick exchange of words, but I didn't quite understand the meaning of "It is too late now." What it actually meant was that Kis Kereszt, my four feet nine inch tall Godmother, and Tomi, my cousin, had been taken from their flat. We learned later that an Arrow Cross lad would have cut off her finger had she not handed over her wedding ring. They were then marched away towards the West. With a considerable bribe, it might just be possible to get them out the column, but there was no time to waste. We hurried back to our flat. Another air raid didn't deter us.

I can only imagine what it was like for Godmother and Tomi. Day after day the column marched four or six abreast in the autumn sunshine, along the dusty main road from Budapest, towards the western border, to Austria. Sunflower fields lay on either side. They passed villagers who were afraid even to offer water to the ailing in the group. And there were guards, guards with rifles, youngsters, completely misled, conditioned and under orders from above.

How did our man know which one to pick out as the subject of his bribe? He must have followed the transport for a long while before he had made his choice. When the time was ripe he acted.

Two people were duly taken aside, turned about, and marched towards yet another unknown destination. When they realised that it was a friend behind the change of direction, I will never know.

What I do know is that there were several days of great apprehension. Nothing was discussed - at least, I did not overhear the adults' conversations.

Then, one afternoon the doorbell rang again. There stood the man I had earlier led to my mother, and behind him Tomi grinned at me. Soon, my Granny and her two daughters were hugging each other, wiping tears away.

Now there were eight of us in our flat. I have no recollection how my mother managed to cope, but she did - as always. Mother, Grandmother and I shared my parents' room, Kis Kereszt and Tomi had my room, and our neighbours must have been put up in the dining room, even though it had no bed or sofa in it. But who cared about such small comforts when life itself was at stake?

The days passed slowly. There was curfew for Jews: they could only leave the building at certain hours of the day, so we did errands for our neighbours. Soon romance blossomed between Tomi and Vera, one of our neighbours. I was the go-between. Tomi was fifteen at the time, seven years my senior. They used to sit next to each other, holding hands in the autumn sunshine on the access balcony. As another diversion Tomi taught me to 'fight' - how to twist an arm behind someone's back or to deliver punches. I was a willing apprentice, since as a child I had sensed my mother always wanted a son. I had even been dressed in boy's clothes up to the age of one. I also learned how to do handstands, with a bit of help, until one day Tomi had dropped me on my head. Some say, I have never recovered.

Sometimes there were raids when Arrow Cross thugs made their way into a flat by kicking in the front door and taking the inhabitants away. We discussed with our neighbours what we should do, in case the Nazis came for them. There was the light well between our flats on first floor level. Bathroom and lavatory windows opened onto it. The lavatory windows were very high up, but the bathroom windows were within reach. It would be possible to climb through and reach the other flat if these were open, so we made a point of keeping them open.

And the Arrow Cross did come one day, looking for Mr Deutsch. While he went to the door, the ladies went to the bathroom and escaped. It all happened very, very quietly. They made it over the drop of one storey into the next flat. We never saw the girls' father again.

Eventually our neighbours went back home, this time through the front door.

My Godmother and Tomi also ventured out, and they went into hiding at Godollo where my other aunt lived. (Grandmother had three daughters.) They did not come back to us till the siege was over.

By Christmas there were only three of us in the flat, my Grandmother, Mother and me. However, we celebrated as well as ever.

On the Continent, presents are received on Christmas Eve and they are usually not wrapped, because presents are directly brought by Baby Jesus, together with the tree. Father and I would be sent out to spend the afternoon away from home while my mother decorated the tree, since children don't see the tree until a bell rings out signalling the arrival of Baby Jesus. We usually had a large tree, reaching up to the high ceiling. The tree was lit, candles on the end of the branches flickered, sparklers sparkled. The surprise was always perfect, even when I didn't believe in the story any more.

That year we had a very small tree, but there were very many books under the tree for me. I hardly had time to open any of them before the sirens screamed to announce another air attack. Soon the concierge called and advised us to leave the flat and move to the cellar, where we all had allocated and prepared quarters. It was in these quarters that we lit real candles to have our Christmas dinner.

Christmas, 1941

I had inherited a set of children's furniture when Tomi had outgrown them: a small, red painted, metal table with two matching chairs. These had been moved down to the cellar for me. I parked my new books on top of each other to take up less space on the table, together with my favourite school books and copybooks. I had my own table, my own light, what more could I want? I was ready for the siege, and I went to bed quite happily between my Mother and Grandmother on the straw filled mattresses made up with our usual bedding.

During the bombing raids, I was not afraid of the actual explosions but one sound did frighten me. In the night, when we heard the dull heavy thumping sound of the aftermath of an explosion, the earth shook a little around us. Coal heaped in the corner started to roll. It was a ghostly, unearthly sound, I can hear it today.

I was busy all the time. Unfortunately, the electricity was cut off, and candles were soon in short supply. I was not allowed my own light, so I had a problem to solve. However, grown ups were willing to let me have their not quite burnt down candles and they saved wax drippings for me. I could melt down this mixture on the stove. My paint set was with me, together with small, round separate dishes. I poured the colourful, messy goo into these and asked Grandmother for something I could use as a wick. In the end I had my very own light supply which lasted to the end of our life in the cellar.

One day I ran crying to my mother, who was standing by the makeshift stove on the half landing leading to the cellars. A range had been installed there to provide some sort of cooking facility for the people now living in the cellars. The range hissed and smoked as new logs were pushed into its belly. Mother seemed to be cooking something, but her gaze was far away. She stood very still, and I did not realise she had tears in her eyes.

"Mummy, someone told me Daddy has been seen around here and in the Basilica at the end of our road," I sobbed. "They are saying Daddy is not away with the army. It isn't true, is it?"

Now she put down the wooden spoon and gathered me in her arms. "People talk; they say all sorts of unpleasant things to me, too. But never mind, little one, it won't be long now. It will come out all right in the end." Eventually, she managed to comfort me.

Of course I did not know about my parent's complicated arrangement while Daddy was in hiding. They used to meet in one of the side chapels of the Basilica at the end of our street hoping not to be discovered. They both risked everything: capture for my Father and our own false sense of security. The white crosses stuck on our windows indicating a Christian family would not have saved us. My mother wasn't Jewish herself, but she was married to a Jew.

And so, hugging each other, we walked back into the dark depth of our corner in the cellar where Granny sat by candlelight, oblivious to all this, playing her never ending card games to see what the future would hold.

Christmas, 1947

After the War

I don't think my Granny could have ever imagined in her wildest dreams, nor would the cards give her the answer to what the future had in store.

The first Russian soldiers arrived, and only a few hours later my father arrived too. (As an adult, I hate to think how other families must have felt witnessing our reunion.) He was alive and well, carrying a large chunk of horse meat. The meatloaf my mother prepared from it became legendary. Everybody in the building had a piece and some people came and kissed her hands. People were more or less starving.

For a while we continued to live in the cellar of our building. Neatly piled logs, or heaps of coal separated us from the neighbours. My father immediately inspected our first floor flat and found it safe to use, although without windows. These were soon boarded up, and it did not take him long to find some glass for replacements. Eventually we moved out of the cellar.

The first wave of Russian soldiers came and went. I remember that they only wanted watches and spirits. Having got these, they were kind to the children, and we had our first Hershey Chocolate Bars. No doubt the Americans were feeding their allies. However, things got worse and we heard of rapes and other atrocities. Raids by soldiers happened regularly. Once back in our flat, we thought it safer to make it look worse than it was. To deter them from entering, our front door was barricaded with odd bits of scaffolding, quite easily found scattered around the streets in those days. Road clearance work was a long way away.

My cousin Tomi and my Godmother came back to us from hiding in Godollo. They could not go home to the other side of the river because the bridges were blown up. Tomi and I were always very fond of each other, in spite of our age gap. Both of us were only children.

One evening it was getting rather late and dark. I was in bed, and was alone in the flat. The grown ups had just gone out to one of our needy neighbours. They hardly ever went anywhere else in those days. There was nowhere to go. The capital was in the process of being "liberated".

For a while I read by the light of my candle, and then I became aware of noises. I could not be sure if it was from the corridor leading to our flat, or from the front door. The noises came nearer and I heard them distinctly. It was our front door. It sounded as if somebody was trying to remove the barricade, but wasn't quite sure how to do it.

"It can't be my parents - they know how to get through without any hassle!" was my first uneasy thought. I put out my candle, even though it would not have been possible to see the light from the front door. "What next? What on earth can I do if it is one of those raiders? Not much!" I was getting frightened.

"At least they don't kill," I thought. "Not children, anyway." Although we were quite grown up in many ways in those days, at the age of not quite nine the meaning of rape was not yet clear to me. The footsteps came nearer, and I felt suddenly very cold and started to shake.

"Perhaps he will think the place is empty, and will go away without noticing me." I tried hard to think of comforting possibilities. "Even if he loots things from the flat he might not notice me in my parents' big bed," and I dived right under my duvet, from where I could watch, unobserved.

The large double door to the room opened, slowly, tentatively. I learned the feel of cold sweat. By now I was paralysed with fear and could not move. A strange taste was in my mouth.

Then, suddenly, in the not quite darkness I recognised the familiar form of my cousin. "Tomi, it is you!" I cried out. And it was. He had tried to come in as quietly as possible not to wake me up, but he had not quite learned the trick with the front door yet, and so he fumbled with it like a stranger. I sobbed with relief – I was never more pleased to see him.

One by one our neighbours arrived back home. Some had left to escape from the advancing Russians army; others had been deported by the Nazis and never made it back home. All were emaciated. Our first priority was food, then the restoration of the flats. Everybody helped. Now that there were another two men in the flats they put a small van together and started to go to the country for food. Some of their adventures were nerve-racking but they always came back with something. We never starved.

From September, 1944, until Spring 1945, schools were closed in Budapest. They reopened soon after the Russian 'liberators' chased out all the Germans. When my school opened they ran out of fuel within days, and there was no heating. The large black stove stood in the corner, towering above us, but there were no comforting red flames showing through from its grate. In the mornings we were cold, and the school was on the verge of closing down again. Then, one day, during our morning break, we were sitting and eating our elevenses in our overcoats when the classroom door opened, and my father's familiar figure appeared. In his black, fur cap and heavy overcoat he looked even stockier than he really was. He carried a very large laundry basket full of firewood. Our cellar was full of firewood, my mother had stocked up in the autumn anticipating the siege and shortage of fuel in the capital.

I didn't know what to make of this. Did my teacher know what was happening? I don't think we were an unusually school-loving class, but spontaneous applause and cheering followed. We had enough logs for a day or two, and after this the school had its own deliveries.

Life went on, and the curriculum for the months we had missed had to be crammed into what was left of the school year. I don't know how, but our teachers did it. We all passed from year three to four by the end of June.

By now we were allowed to walk home on our own. One day while we walked I tried to make sure my friends the twins would come over to my house later in the afternoon. It would be so sad not to have one of our games today, perhaps a special birthday game of Monopoly, for this was my first birthday after the war.

Not much had been said about it, and I had no expectations of treats. School lasted from eight to twelve, and lunch at home was as usual. I had already received my presents in the morning, before school. They were laid out at the foot of my bed, and I was happily discovering the ins and outs of them when the surprise event began. The doorbell went, and in quick succession members of my family and friends arrived. In my parents' room, the top of the baby grand piano was soon full of goodies and presents.

Granny looked very pleased: her snow white hair had quite a radiance about it, which contrasted well with her dark dress with small white patterns. Isn't it strange? I remember her clearly, but I cannot recall my own dress.

One of the grown-ups soon organised a traditional game of tombola. Little did we know that bingo would take over and commercialise our childish entertainment. Everybody won something to take home.

Next, we went into our dining room, all of us seated around the large, oval dining room table. Its beautiful mahogany top was protected with a felt like cover and a starched, white damask tablecloth. Little open sandwiches and drinks were laid out on it, together with sweets.

My father got busy with his camera. The set of shallow drawers slid out from behind the doors of the large sideboard, and he took out all the attachments. Finally, he was ready with his flash and tripod, and he made sure he would be on the picture. Then the large glazed double doors opened, and a cake lit with ten candles was brought in. Everybody clapped, the camera clicked and I blew out the candles.

At the end of year four a big decision had to be made about choice of school. My parents muttered quite a lot about which school I should attend. It was important, because I would stay for the next eight years in the school, up to A levels, a French style baccalaureate. There was no question about not going for it.

Of course, my parents wanted the best for their one and only daughter. Although we were not really religious they chose the Lutheran school (Evangélikus Gimnázium.) I liked my school and I was not aware that children of different religions paid different fees. Years and years later my great friends the twins told me about this. I sat on the same bench as Eva for the next three years, and we are still friends today

My cousin Tomi was now in his seventh year at the boy's school of the same establishment. We had only one more year left when we coincided, so I made the most of it. There were dancing lessons if you wanted to learn, and at age eleven I had a smashing partner in him, no doubt to the envy of some of the others.

When we were 12 or 13 years old, four of us used to walk home together. The twins Eva and Vera and their cousin Nora lived in the same house in O-utca, just one street away from my house. The other Eva lived a bit further away in a similar block of flats to ours. She was Jewish, and later joined a Zionist organisation. When her group was ready to leave Hungary for Israel her parents would not allow her to go. On the day of the group's departure Eva threw herself off the third floor courtyard balcony of their block. She did not survive.

On our way home from school we had to cross the inner boulevard with the tramlines in the middle. One day Nora announced, "They have a paternoster lift in the bank." We knew the building - it was on our way home from school when we crossed Governor Joseph's Square. (Jozsef Nádor ter). We passed Governor Joseph's statue in the middle of the square at the centre of a grassed patch, protected by a low, very heavy decorative chain fence fixed to massive pillars at each corner. We used to swing on these.

"How do you know?"

"What is a paternoster lift?" we asked in unison.

"I was there with my parents." She was quite excited. "It has no doors and it doesn't stop. You have to jump in and out."

We couldn't quite believe this.

"All right, let's go in and try it one day."

"But will children be allowed to go inside the Hungarian National Bank?" We had some doubts.

Nora came up with a bright idea. "If we speak English among ourselves, they will not understand us, and they will not be able to send us away."

We had all chosen to learn English as our foreign language at school. It was 1948, and Russian had not yet become compulsory. Some of us also had private lessons and we were very proud of ourselves being at the top of the class.

We entered the ornate classical building. No one stopped us, and we reached the lifts on the right hand side of the banking hall. Here the fun started. A most fascinating type of lift faced us. The Paternoster got its name because its cabins resembled to Catholic confession booths. It was an endless chain of such booths, which were constantly in motion, rolling up one shaft and down another. You had to jump on and off the small open-fronted cabins as they approached your floor to avoid being scissored as the booths passed to the floor above or below you. You could also ride downwards in this delightful contraption. Stiletto heels were not fashionable in those days. I hate to think what could have happened if anyone got caught wearing these.

One of these cabins could comfortably accommodate two or three of us. We happily jumped in and out on several floors, trying not to make too much noise. Our after-school entertainment lasted perhaps half an hour, and we became quite addicted. Day after day we marched in as if we really had some business there, talking in English – or so we thought - quite expecting to be stopped and thrown out before we could reach the relative safety of the lift. Sometimes we even sat down on our school bags in the cabin, and I began to wonder what it was like at the upper and lower turn-around points. The others took a lot of convincing to ride up with me all the way to the top. The machine drew us up into total darkness as we trundled, wobbling, over the upper wheels then were sent down again into the adjacent descending shaft. I must confess I was a bit worried that we would be turned upside down as we went over the top, but eventually we became quite blasé about the experience. But we never tried the bottom turn-around and we were never caught.

These years were very busy. I was doing quite a lot of figure skating, and I was learning to play the piano. I was allowed time off from school to train. This resulted in my school marks dropping. My parents were not too pleased, and I remember thinking this was quite unfair. I did not realise then my parents' high expectations of me.

My father loved skating, but he couldn't persuade my mother to learn. So when I was old enough, he taught me. There was only one ice rink in Budapest with artificial ice. It was a lake in the summer with boating for the public. At the edge of the lake stood a slightly curved building which contained the boathouse and changing rooms. Above was the entrance from the road with a spacious foyer. The ticket office, a medical suite, offices, and a way to the restaurant opened from the foyer, and two curved flights of steps led downstairs to the level of lake.

Skating wasn't a sport the regime supported. It was an individual, bourgeois sport which had to be heavily subsidised by the parents. It didn't fit in with the communist ideology. Those who got to the top took part in international competitions travelling within the communist countries. When they were allowed to compete in the West, many of them didn't return, risking their family's arrest at home. But this was their only way to get out of the country.

After a few lessons I was able to stand on my feet and do a few basic moves. Then my father, an 'ice dad' who dreamt that his daughter would become a figure skater, employed a trainer. Uncle Sanyi was an old-fashioned gentleman, and he looked very old to me. He never put on skates, but slid over the ice in shoes covered in some kind of felt. During my training sessions, and afterwards when I was practising, my father, who was a reasonable ice-dancer, used to have a couple of dances with various ladies There was music playing all the time. Then he sat in the upstairs restaurant with Uncle Sanyi. They smoked and drank mulled wine, and they also watched me from up there.

There was usually an area set aside for the figure skaters in the middle of the ice rink, where I practised, surrounded by 'ice-mums' who were watching their daughters. These were mothers whose own youthful dreams had not come true. Now they closely guarded their daughters, standing by the railings of our enclosure in their fur lined boots stamping their feet in the cold. For hours and hours they watched their own daughters like hawks, and spied on all the others from the corner of their eyes. I was the odd one out, who hardly ever had her mother around.

We could not practise elsewhere, although the rink was large. The middle was artificial ice and that ensured a season from early December to the end of

February. When it turned really cold the rest of the lake froze over and there was plenty of room. The speed skaters circled round and round and they didn't take much notice of us. But the members of the hockey team were shockers. One of their favourite occupations was to trip us up and then to catch us. I had long plaits, nearly down to my bottom. They liked to grab one or both of them, trip me over and then hold out an arm to catch me falling. Being caught by just one plait was rather painful. I complained, but my father wouldn't hear of having my hair cut, he must have liked long hair. I heard he nearly broke off their engagement when my mother had hers cut off. When I was spinning, my plaits spread out horizontally and looked fine, but at other times they just added to the danger of being caught. By now I was a junior figure skater.

One night there was no dancing or training. It was the night of the big event, the championships. The whole rink was a stage, with stands erected on two sides for the spectators. The announcement for the start of the free skating programmes of the national championship came.

Music played. The beginners started. We, the juniors were to follow. The compulsory figures had been skated the day before. I always did well in this section I took to the compulsory figures like a duck to water. It was thrilling to carve those figures eights, threes, double threes and loops on to the clean ice. I gained my points doing those, only to be left behind when it came to free skating. That wasn't my scene. Both as a beginner, and later, as a junior, I always slipped into third position behind the same two contemporaries.

My main rival Hedy Pálinkás was about my height and build. I knew she would overtake me, her programme was more difficult than mine and she oozed confidence. Her jumps were better; she could do one and a half turns in one of them. I could only manage one. But I was good at the pirouettes, high or low, my two long plaits spread out and stole the show.

Marietta was quite different. She was tall for her age and very slim. Sometimes she could not make up for the points I gained at the compulsories and I came second. Her free skating wasn't as good as Hedy's but still better than mine. However, she was temperamental, and she could spoil movements when they most mattered. She was not a good competitor. Her parents were quite friendly with my father. It was her mother who mostly accompanied her, and she often sat in the upstairs restaurant with my father overlooking the rink. They drank their interminable black coffees and sometimes something stronger to warm up. It must have cost quite a lot, not to mention all those private lessons we had.

Wrapped in our overcoats, we dutifully practised and prepared for the big event. When the time came, we went through the now empty changing room to our enclosure. We had to go through the lady's area to a special little enclosure for the figure skaters. It was quite hot and steamy in there. Low benches lined the walls, under the built-in lockers, where we competition dancers kept our gear. The general public carried their skates, which were fixed onto their ordinary high lace up shoes with a special key. *We* had purpose made skating boots with the skates permanently fixed to them. Today the enclosure was buzzing. As the beginners finished, the juniors arrived, complete with the army of ice-mothers. I never had anyone with me there. I sometimes wished my old Uncle Sanyi was a woman. This was the moment when we first saw each other's dresses. On this occasion, Hedy, at age 12 and already glamorous, was wearing a gold threaded dress. Where on earth did they get hold of such a material, in the second season after the war, when hardly anything was available? It must have come from the West. Neither did we have tights in those days. We practised in trousers or bare legs beneath our skirts. And we didn't feel the cold! Or so we thought. Marietta was in a simple, lightweight navy outfit, a pleated skirt and just a little white trimming on her blouse. She looked elegant.

Hedy, our trainer, Marietta, myself

It was time to put on those white boots. My first pair. I had wanted them for a long time: it took me so long to grow out of the old brown pair. I liked to think my skating improved with the new, 'real' boots. I tightened my laces, hooked around the shiny buttons, and tied them around the boot above my ankle. The first girl had already left the dressing room: her programme would only take three minutes, then the judges would take their time to give their verdict. One could certainly not relax in the changing room.

Hedy was about to leave. She looked wonderful in her glittering gold dress. As she stretched to put on her coat, she sort of tripped as if one leg didn't work. Surprised, she sat down to see what the matter was. Her mother was there already. Nothing hurt, and the boot was done up properly. Then somebody next to her pointed to one of her skates. There was a thin line on the blade, a crack. Had it been sawn across? We all kept our skates in the changing room, never took them home. Anyway, she couldn't skate.

The announcement came, and I had to go. I went through my programme, not very well. I knew I would slip to the second place, but this was not the way I hoped to have the glory as runner up in the competition. There were no prizes, but the leaders were promoted

Then one winter I had an accident. After a split jump I landed badly and one skate cut into my other calf. The duty doctor immediately clipped the cut and they phoned for my mother. She came and took me home. There was no fuss or tears, but unfortunately I developed complications, and by the time I could skate again, the others were even more advanced. In the relatively short period when we could skate, one could not afford to miss out for weeks on end. I was left behind, and I didn't have the enthusiasm to continue without my father pushing me. I was 14 years old, and my mother allowed me to have my plaits cut off. My father was not in a position to object. He was in prison.

It happened during a shooting weekend, when a small party went out in my father's car. A friend was driving, and my father was in the back with his mistress. I knew, and even liked the lady in question, whom I had met socially, though I had no idea what was going on. They had an accident, and they didn't report it at the time. Some time later, the police caught up with them. They wanted my father to admit that he was the driver, but he refused, though during the interrogation his hair turned white overnight. He was sentenced to a year's imprisonment; his friend got four years.

A year or so later, my father and I went to the rink a couple of times, we had a dance and a drink together, but my skating career was over.

Me after the war

In later years I played the usual team games at school. It earned me badly needed brownie points. Netball and volley ball were not frowned upon, and I loved the team spirit. There were no politics in ball games. Tennis was, of course, condemned as completely bourgeois. No wonder there wasn't a single Hungarian international player until the late sixties. With my background I couldn't afford even try it, as much as I would have loved to.

In 1949 or 1950 the government passed new legislation and raised the school leaving age to be fourteen, and unfortunately obliged everybody to attend the school in their own district. I had to transfer to a school which had been run by Catholic nuns before they were banned from education and the convents were abolished. I didn't like this establishment at all. It was in this school that I was coerced into the Pioneer organisation. My form teacher called me aside, and told me in no uncertain terms that if I wanted to carry on studying I had better join. I did.

At fourteen years of age I finished my eight years of compulsory education with 'A' plus results. I wanted to go for the next four years to a school which prepared students for A levels but which also had courses in architecture and building to a technician's level. I used to like geometry homework when we had to use rulers to draw shapes. My mother once mentioned in passing that I could perhaps become an architect. The idea stuck. If I didn't qualify to go to university from this school, at least I would have some qualification.

The system thought otherwise. They allocated me to an ordinary grammar school. I refused to go, saying that I would not continue studying at all, unless I could go where I wanted to. And having said that, I went off to Lake Balaton where I joined family friends to spend the summer. I swam, cycled, or danced the night away with my seniors, who used me as go-between while carrying on their romances. I thoroughly enjoyed myself.

My father was not available for consultation, being in prison after the unpleasant events surrounding that car accident, so during the summer my mother worked behind the scenes. Her efforts resulted in a piece of paper informing me that I could now enrol at another school with special subjects in building services. I still objected, and waited until the beginning of the school year when I marched up to my chosen school. They had a vacancy, of course, and enrolled me.

So in September my secondary education began in the Technicum, a coeducational school where I made new friends. One of them was Ivan. He had wanted to go to a Grammar School, so he was allocated to my chosen establishment. He was short, stocky and rather scruffy. He had specs. I was slightly taller, sporty, and my mother saw to it that I was well dressed. Ivan had a crush on me, and it wasn't reciprocated. He was like a fish out of water. He had dreamt of journalism and politics, but not the politics of the current regime. His mother was not a fighter, and his journalist father was not on the scene, so Ivan enrolled. He was totally unsuited to technical subjects. I used to help him out, and sometimes did his homework. We struck up a friendship, based on how much we were out of tune with communist Hungary.

He always had some excuse to go home my way, even though he lived in quite a different direction. On our way we made endless jokes about our teachers. 'Green Jacket' was one of our favourite butts. He was our Russian teacher, who always wore a rather bright green jacket. I learned decades later from his younger brother that his real subjects were Latin and Hungarian, but he had to learn Russian, just ahead of us to be able to remain in teaching. Often, Ivan and I would share a cup of coffee on our way home - we could not afford one each.

Then in our second year Ivan was expelled and simply disappeared. No one knew why he had gone, and no one stood up for him. My father, on the other hand, bribed the caretaker with boxes of cigars to save me from reprimand for being late too often. At the same time, however, my pocket money was reduced to a minimum until the caretaker reported more favourably about me.

I settled in the new school. On the 21st December the headmaster held an assembly in the school's spacious entrance hall, decorated by the bust of Comrade Stalin. We used to stand on parade by this bust for a whole hour at a time, holding a lit torch to celebrate his birthday.

Another assembly was all about preparations for the march on the 1st May. The whole country would march, complete with banners, smiling faces and unbridled enthusiasm. Our school would be one of many. Of course we all had to take part. Absentees would need a sick note. We would meet an hour earlier than usual for school. The route we were to take was outlined by the headmaster, who had his instructions from higher authorities. All was to be very spontaneous, you understand, as it was to be reported by the censored media.

May 1st dawned. It was spring, with temperatures between 18-20 centigrade. My new dress, a red tartan check, with short sleeves, awaited me. We had no uniforms. I don't know why my mother had chosen the red material, she was no fan of the regime, but it was a nice dress, and I was pleased with it. What was more, I thought the colour, politically so correct, might earn me some badly needed brownie points. My behaviour was not exactly exemplary in school during these years - only my study results saved me from disgrace.

It was not cold, even at seven o'clock in the morning, when we duly met in the school. As we started walking it got even warmer. Four abreast, with stop and go type progress for a couple of miles, we followed the waves of demonstrators in front of us, all the way to Stalin's much larger than life statue in City Park. Dignitaries stood at his feet like minions, and waved to us as we marched past. What fun! we thought ironically, but no one dared to say anything. Then it was all over, and we were quite lucky to be free by early afternoon. The rest of the day was ours, to play or picnic in the park with a minimum of supervision. We were not tired - we didn't know the meaning of that word yet. But I was feeling hot, very hot. Perhaps it was due to the ball games.

As more and more people arrived in the park it was becoming crowded, so we decided to call it a day, and left for home. Quite a journey lay ahead of us, through diversions and streets closed to normal traffic. The march was more important than people.

When I got home, my mother took one look at me and fetched the thermometer. I was normally pale and she didn't like my rosy cheeks or my unusually bright eyes. My temperature soared. Very quickly I was put to bed. By next morning spots appeared, and they confirmed I had chickenpox.

My schoolmates used to come to visit me. I looked through the first floor window, and they talked to me from the street below. The neighbours must have enjoyed some of the school gossip. My best consolation during the following three weeks of isolation was a white hyacinth, the first flower I ever received from a young man. It stood on my bedside table, and ever since I have loved its scent.

Life before the Revolution

After my parents' divorce I lived with my mother, in our old flat. I considered myself as my mother's knight in shining armour, and I was unforgiving as far as my father was concerned. However, we met weekly, and I behaved as badly as a reasonably intelligent teenager could.

About a year later a new legislation came into force about the size of flats. My mother and I were no longer allowed the large apartment we occupied. The authorities could plant somebody else in our flat at any time. I persuaded my mother we should rather let my old room to one of my school friends. Bandi Soltész was one year ahead of me at school, and was two years older than me. As well as attending school, he worked part time at the building of the new underground. It was dangerous work, and he got extra food rations which he often brought back to us.

Of course, the inevitable followed, and we decided to announce our engagement on my 16th birthday. It was 1952, the year Comrade Stalin died. No one knew exactly when or how the dictator died, but his death was announced on my birthday. The city had black flags everywhere. I would never have believed that my sixteenth birthday would be so memorable – even without our engagement!

There was no thought of cancelling the celebration. Aunts and uncles arrived, Granny was radiant again, and my best friends the twins were there too. The black piano was covered in flowers. Champagne flowed, instead of the childish juices of previous occasions. I did not like the taste of champagne. I was obviously not ready for it, nor for many other things. But I bravely clinked my glass with my fiancé's, and with everyone else's afterwards. Smiles, kisses and tear-filled eyes followed us.

"Of course, they are too young!" We could hear the whispers not intended for our ears.

The large white double doors opened, and an enormous cake was brought in. Elegant candles burnt around the writing: "Congratulations! Long live the bride of 16."

At the tender ages of 17 and 19 respectively, we were married in a civil ceremony, on the morning of New Years Eve, 1953. By this time, my husband had finished school, and he was working. But no one believed this marriage would be "Till death do us part." Even then, I knew that I should not have married him. In no time at all our marriage was on the rocks, and by the summer of 1954 we were divorced.

By June 1953, I had done my A levels, with top marks in everything except one subject. It had been a standing joke during the school year that I didn't like, and didn't know the ins and outs of paints. At the oral exam my teacher handed me a paper on that particular subject. I handed it back. But however well I knew whatever the next subject might be, I could no longer get top marks. That was that. I had blown my university entry. With top marks in every subject a student entered university automatically. I had to take the entrance examinations. I passed them, but there were other considerations. With my middle class, bourgeois background, I was refused a place. I started work, but I also took private lessons in physics, which was my weakest subject, thinking of the following year's entrance exams. I tried again, and again got top marks - but again, excuses were made, and I was refused a place.

First Wedding

The days of persecution and deportations were with us for a long time. The 1945 'liberators' of the country transferred all power to the previously illegal communists, whose leaders had been in exile in the Soviet Union, and had come back with the Red Army tanks. There was one free election, but the communists did not win, and it was soon forgotten. I was made to realise that I was a middle class enemy alien. The slogan was that "bourgeois parasites" (as we were referred to) should be alienated, separated, eliminated - preferably eliminated. There were plenty of examples in recent history of how to do it. Stalin and his henchmen had learned much from Hitler.

Many families, professionals or those owning small businesses, lived in cramped one-room accommodation, their houses and flats confiscated, their assets nationalised. Like my father's business, and his car. At best, the owner was employed to run his own plant for a while, until a politically more reliable person could be found. Eight or nine years earlier, the Nazi persecution had generated similar fear. I could remember it. Now, we were experiencing something quite similar. Nightly, or at crack of dawn, doorbells rang, and uniformed secret police entered, to give families less than an hour to pack their belongings. Most of us kept a suitcase packed, as if we were going to hospital - except that this time it would be deportation. Usually, people were taken from the city to far away hamlets, or farms at the back of beyond. Everything was the back of beyond for us city dwellers with absolutely no experience how to till the soil. The houses were primitive, to say the least, with rammed earth floors, and with no sanitation.

I was feeling pretty low when one evening my mother gave me her ticket to a play to cheer me up and to get me out of the house. In the interval of the performance, I became aware of somebody watching me. You know how girls notice things even with their heads turned away. I turned to look. Our eyes met, and that was all. I looked away, but could not help a quick mental note of how handsome the observer was. The play, which I thoroughly enjoyed, ended with many curtain calls and a standing ovation. Nobody was in a hurry to reach for coats and to leave.

It was cold outside: fur coats and winter wraps were the order of the evening. On the way to the theatre I had had to take the tram in order not to be late, so a leisurely walk home was welcome. It would take me perhaps twenty or twenty five minutes. In my nice burgundy coloured overcoat and matching burgundy coloured shoes, I felt quite chic as I strolled along the main boulevard on my way home, along streets lined with well lit shops just right for window shopping. Shoe shops, in particular, were always my favourites. As I examined a rather nice black pair and contemplated how many months of savings they would cost me, I noticed the face

I had seen in the theatre reflected in the glass. He was alone, too. I ignored him, as if the shops were more interesting. He overtook me, and then fell behind - several times. It was becoming a game. There were places where we both stopped and looked intently at whatever the shop had on display. And we smiled. We could not help smiling and looking at each other. The situation was becoming quite ridiculous.

When I reached the turning for my side street I wondered what to do. I did not want him to follow me right up to my home, but I was ready for a bit of an adventure. At a jeweller's shop window where we both stopped again, as if we could be interested in anything as expensive as the displayed pieces, I turned sideways and boldly announced: "I don't normally play games like this, but hello! Let's get introduced."

He was not in the least taken aback. Smiling, he held out his hand, and we quite formally introduced ourselves: Gábor Pinter-Kovàcs and Àgi Wohl. He was tall, very tall, and now I could see those eyes were very blue. Conversation came easily: we discussed the play we had just seen. Eventually, I wanted to make my excuses, and I said: "I live just here around the corner, so - so long."

"Do you really want to go home already?" he asked. "There is a small patisserie open across the road. We could have a coffee." So we did. By the time he took me home it was nearly midnight, and he asked if he could see me again.

"Of course, ring me up some time," and I gave him my phone number.

He rang quite soon, and we got into the habit of dating. We had a lot in common in our backgrounds, not to mention mutual physical attraction. Gábor was 24, a mature student. After his A levels he had been refused higher education, as he was middle class, his father a doctor and a small landowner. He was therefore an enemy alien. A few years later he was admitted to university, only to be thrown out at the end of the second year during one of the purges. We had thus shared very similar experiences, and reacted to them in a similar way. We certainly understood each other.

A few more weeks passed. On Saturdays we danced late in fashionable night clubs or went to the pictures and had a drink or coffee at my place. We were not quite ready to introduce each other to family and friends. One weekday evening we met at a wine bar near his home on the other side of the river. We had had quite a bit to drink, and not much food. It didn't matter in those days, as youngsters had no cars to drive. We certainly had not. We used to walk home. Gàbor later bought a motor bike - a status symbol But that evening, he said he planned to show me his home. Would I come?

Life before the Revolution

"No one will be in," he mentioned casually.

That's a change! I thought, and I was quite excited about it.

By now I knew he had a sister a little younger than me. We walked to the darkened entrance of a small, modern block of flats in a posh area. The whole building had been owned by his father, before the new regime 'nationalised' it. They had been allowed to keep the penthouse flat, though it was not large enough for a family of four. However, the two big rooms, a room for the parents, and another for the 'children', both furnished with antiques, opened from a hexagonal hall. They were more than many other people had in those days. Gabor opened the door to a rather long room with a large bay window overlooking the park below. A concealed door, decorated the same way as the walls, led to a bathroom, as I later discovered. The room we were in was a serious room, with a beautiful, large writing desk polished to perfection, and brown leather seating. It was clear that sister and brother had to share the same room. Three-seater convertible sofas doubling as beds were arranged at each end of the room to give maximum privacy possible under the circumstances. On one of them was scattered some girl's clothing, as if somebody had left in a hurry. An aura of student existence lingered in the air. I liked it.

There was more wine, but still nothing to eat. My tummy began to feel funny. The nice well-ordered room appeared to be moving. I was dizzy. "My goodness, I've never been drunk before - can it be like this?" I wondered. I said nothing. After all, perhaps his arms around me were making me dizzy. It got worse, until I had to excuse myself. Luckily I found the concealed bathroom door in time.

Both Gabor's family and mine were in constant fear of deportation. On days when we didn't meet, he developed a habit of ringing me at 10 o'clock in the evening. I could set my watch by these calls. He knew I would be in bed, nearly falling asleep, with the phone at my bedside. It was quite a luxury to sink into slumber after a fond good night call. I was used to my 10 o'clock calls, and was not even surprised at first when the bell rang, although by then I had been asleep for some time. I slowly came to, and picked up the phone. It was dead. The ringing was the doorbell, and it was nearly midnight. Frozen with horror, I listened to my mother's footsteps as she walked down the hall. Had they come for us? Would they knock down the door?

I heard the door opening - voices. That was our neighbour! What could she want at this time of the night? I climbed out of bed to look out into the hall. In the doorway stood Mrs Deutsch, with her two daughters behind her – those same daughters who had climbed to safety from our bathroom so many years ago. Behind the girls, I could just make out a man in uniform, shifting impatiently from one foot to the other.

"Now!" he insisted.

My mother hugged our neighbours, and then watched as they were marched away. We had helped them to escape from the Nazis, but there was no escape this time. They were deported. We were lucky that neither we nor Gábor's family were deported.

In the summer of 1955 my mother saw a travel advertisement. This was something quite unusual. The Hungarian riverboat company which ran a regular service up and down the Danube advertised a trip to the South, to Yugoslavia and part of Romania. My mother and Kis Kereszt were quite enthusiastic about it, and I was invited, too. My first trip abroad! None of us had individual passports, we travelled on a communal document, and we were definitely not encouraged to go ashore on our own anywhere. The Hungarian stretch of the river runs through quite flat countryside, it is slow and very wide. Towards Belgrade the scenery changes, the banks close up, and the river flows fast. At the Iron Gate there are high cliffs on both sides. The river was not navigable beyond here until the end of the 19th century, when a passage was cut.

We arrived in Belgrade. It looked vibrant and Westernised compared with Budapest. A young man was there to meet me, the brother of Nikolaj, a Yugoslav acquaintance of ours in Budapest. Nikolaj travelled regularly between Belgrade, Budapest and Vienna, and he was quite ready to make arrangements for me not to return to the boat. However, after having been wined and dined, I chickened out of this arrangement. I was worried what would happen to my mother and to Kis Kereszt if I didn't return, and after all, Yugoslavia was not my dream place to escape to. Besides, there was Gábor. So I went tamely back to the boat, where I was anxiously awaited. One stop further on we saw an old spa in Romania. The people there were very poor, even poorer than the Hungarians. In the boat's communal dormitory that night I whispered to my elders of the adventures I had back in Belgrade. I had been impressed, but I returned home.

The year slowly dragged on. A New Year's Eve party was planned at a friend's house, where the parents had gone out. Eventually it came to climax: the dance music stopped, and the radio announced midnight. Then twelve strokes of a bell welcomed in the New Year. After clinking our glasses, we all piled into the steamy kitchen, where a large saucepan full of water was on the boil. Traditionally, people had to make a wish before throwing a drop of lead into the steaming cauldron. There it would take some shape - anything from a wedding cake, a Parker pen or a boat - to be interpreted by us. This was supposed to indicate what the next year would hold for the person, reflecting whatever was uppermost in his or her mind.

My turn came and I made no wish. There was such a lot I could wish for, so I could not choose. I just waited for the silvery, grey mess to take some shape. Then, with a wooden spoon, I lifted it out of the water for everyone to see. A unanimous muffled cry went up. It was a tank. The year was 1956.

And one afternoon towards the end of that year came rumours of a student rally by the Petofi statue on the river bank. The venue was significant, because the 19th century poet personified the struggle for independence from the Austrian Habsburg monarchy.

Although the office building where I worked as a technician was quite near, we didn't actually hear anything. My short walk home from work was uneventful, with the usual crowds hurrying in every direction. Mother arrived soon after me. She had witnessed the gatherings on her way. This was an unusual and strange phenomenon because demonstrations and unofficial gatherings were not allowed.

That evening I was going out again, to have the first fitting for my new coat. A consignment of blue and pink baby blankets had recently arrived from China, and Mother had managed to get hold of a few. Luckily they were blue ones. This meant I could have a new overcoat. On the way to the dressmaker, I had to pass the larger than life statue of Comrade Stalin. There, I had the surprise of my young life. A large crowd was attacking the statue with weapons of every description. They used anything to hand. Then blow torches appeared, brought by factory workers, the privileged class of the regime. This was no student demonstration. This was the beginning of an uprising.

By the time I returned it was dark. The statue at the edge of City Park had been brought down. Stalin lay across the vast paved square, where on 1st May and on 7th November, processions had saluted and passed by him. People took chunks and splinters of the bronze body as mementos of an ugly regime. I took one, too. There was something in the air. The atmosphere was electric, but I went home.

Both Mother and I went to work next morning. News came in flashes - first that the radio building had been taken over by the demonstrators, then news of shooting into the crowds at Parliament Square. The demonstrators were unarmed: all they had were a few flags from which they had cut out the hated red star, so that only the national colours of red, white and green remained, with a hole in the middle. This became the symbol of the revolution. Red stars were falling from the top of buildings, red stars in the October sky.

For a few feverish days we lived in a fool's paradise, believing that the Russian troops would be withdrawn from the country 11 years after of their 'victorious' arrival. It was as if the country had woken up from a bad dream. For many years a single party had been foisted on the people; now the multi-party system of the past reappeared. The Russians had promised to withdraw the army, and for a few days they seemed actually to have done it. Shooting stopped, there was no looting; the revolution was "clean". In no time at all, the offices of the long banned political parties opened up. Those were delirious days. We actually believed freedom had come to stay - that we had actually got away with it. But we hadn't. Our freedom lasted only a few days.

A few mornings later, I woke up to the sound of artillery and the rumbling of very heavy vehicles. My Mother was already up. "It sounds like war," she said, and calmly continued her breakfast. She had had plenty of experience, having gone through the First World War as a young girl, and survived the Second, that time with me, and a husband who had been conscripted into a labour battalion.

"There are Russian tanks in the street," I told her.

"Come away from the window, and leave the curtains alone," she answered.

The Russians returned in full force. The rest is history. The tanks were sent in, and the small Hungarian army was no match for them. Treachery, broken promises - we were back to square one. Worse was to follow. Reprisals came. Anyone who had taken part in the uprising was in danger. But the border to Austria was open, and the Hungarian border guards were on the side of the uprising. The Russians had not yet replaced them.

Ivan appeared one night in spite of the general curfew, complete with his gun. He had been in the fight, and he was on the run.

"I'm leaving," he announced. "I have to. Come with me, and I will get you out of this country."

This was unexpected, and I was taken aback. "I've got to wait," I said.

"What are you waiting for?" He was astonished. "There's no hope. We're completely surrounded by the Soviet Army."

"I'm waiting for Gàbor, my boyfriend. He left for the country and we lost contact. I don't believe he would have left for the West without me. I only hope he has not been rounded up and deported towards Siberia," I replied. "In any case, I want to wait a little longer."

He looked at me long and hard, and slowly said: "I must leave and leave soon, so goodbye."

People were called back to work. Reconstruction started. First, we had to assess damage to the buildings in the city – but on the main roads only. There was no money for the side streets. There, the tell-tale signs of siege remained even ten, fifteen years later. Turning into a side street felt like crossing from East to West Berlin. During the day there was hardly any traffic on the streets. In the evening curfew was imposed, and the city felt dead.

The telephone lines, however, were not damaged, so my father got through to find out if we were all right. He lived a short distance away with his new family - a brisk twenty minutes walk, in the absence of public transport. As it happened, he had been in Czechoslovakia on business when the trouble started, and he had only just managed to get home. As a great treat, he had one single banana, which was shared out between my half-brother Lacko and me. Neither of us had tasted a banana before. They said I had had bananas before the war, but I didn't remember it.

A few weeks passed, and circumstances did not improve. I did not take any active part in the fighting, but helping to burn personal records at the firm I worked for would not do my future much good. Ivan's departure had made me think. How long could I wait? A few more anxious days went by, and I learned that even Gábor's parents did not know of his whereabouts.

So, now or never, was my conclusion. This was my decision, and my mother did not object, unlike some other mothers at that time. She only asked me to discuss it with my father. I thought this was an unbelievable reaction after their divorce, which had not been a friendly one. But I called on my father. I reached his home in daylight, and I explained that I wanted to leave. It would be my only chance to go on studying. He was quiet for a short while, and looked very seriously at me. A little later, he walked back with me in the direction of my home to make sure I reached it before the curfew. Suddenly he stopped, and said, "There is no future for you here. Go." I was just twenty years old.

It was getting dark, and the better part of the walk lay ahead of me. "I think I'll try to hitch-hike from here," I said. He was not too happy, but I was in a hurry because a few days earlier I had been caught after the curfew and had hardly managed to reach our block of flats before a military vehicle rumbled down our street. I was convinced they had noticed me in the distance, and it was touch and go if I could get inside the big wooden gates in time. I did.

Tomi leaves for Switzerland

47

So that night, although I certainly would not have ridden in a Russian vehicle, when a Hungarian military car approached I tried my luck. My father quizzed them about where were they were going. I just got in. There was one empty seat at the back, among the three officer-types. I had never learned to recognise the ranks. They duly dropped me off, and I got home as planned. My mother's first words were, "Your father just rang. He forgot something. He wants you to call him back." He had not forgotten anything at all, he was simply worried about my rather unusual mode of transport and the company I had kept.

I spent my last night in Hungary in my room, in the company of my best friend, Eva, one of the Robert twins. We packed my sports bag. I was to leave next morning, on the 30th November, to board a train bound for the western border. I had had to forge a document which would allow me to enter the Austrian border zone, otherwise I could have easily been returned before I got anywhere. Eva wanted to come too, but her mother would not let her, threatening to jump from the second floor if Eva left. Curled up at each end of my sofa, we selected pictures from my photo album which I wanted to take with me. I even included one of Comrade Stalin, to prevent homesickness!

Two hundred thousand refugees escaped from Hungary that year, out of a total of ten million inhabitants. And so did I - but without my new blue overcoat.

A Little Dagger and a Big Bottle

At the railway station my father was already on the platform. It was cold, and he had on his heavy, fur lined overcoat and his small black fur cap - the sort shepherds used to have. He had come to see me off, and he had not come empty handed. He had already paid the fee to the guide who was to take a group across the Russian patrolled border. Some people got rich in those days. Now he took a large, litre bottle of schnapps from inside his coat and handed it to me. That was not all. Something small followed, which at first I could not quite make out. It was a slim, grey leather sleeve containing a small dagger, with a horn handle and brass decorations. The blade was shiny, though not new, and it was very sharp. I looked a question mark at him. "Should you find yourself in difficulties, one or the other might help. Use them." And he slid both his farewell gifts into the sports bag which now contained all my worldly belongings.

The train was packed with would-be refugees, although we did not, of course, know each other. A man who was to be our guide made himself known by telling us the name of the station where we were to alight. I could scarcely wait. At last the train drew into the station. Lots of us got off, and we quickly and quietly drew together into small groups.

"Next stop, Austria," joked the ticket collector as we passed the barrier.

We left the station, and walked for miles, deep into the forest, until we arrived at our guide's house. There we waited – many anxious hours it seemed – until it was time for the routine change of guards. Normally the border was patrolled by Russian guards, but from time to time a detachment of Hungarian guards would take this duty. Then we could escape. Meanwhile, however, we were treated to glasses of gluhwein, and worn out by tension and excitement, I fell asleep.

We set out again - a small group of about sixteen people. Among us was my Uncle Pista, who had recently returned from the Soviet Union where he had spent many years as a prisoner of war. We all carried some baggage. My sports bag, which was all I had, was not heavy. When I slipped on an icy patch, covered with fallen leaves and hurt my ankle, my uncle offered to carry it for me. Pain or no pain, there was no stopping.

We had to reach the end of the thickly wooded patch. Towards the edge, we were told to expect a clearing and a road. The road would have a bend in it, alongside a stone wall and fields on the other side. Past the wall, it would be all over. We would have crossed the border.

It was getting lighter. The moon became visible, and spread a silvery gleam over the emerging landscape. We had just reached the end of the thickly wooded patch. Now we were walking on the road, and I limped at the back. The others turned the bend, by a wall. Suddenly, I noticed a light on the stones of the wall. "Someone's coming! Watch out!" I cried.

The light became sharper and the very distant rumble of a vehicle was just audible - an armoured car.

"Get off the road! Hide in the fields!" someone shouted.

We scattered. The group disappeared, some into the field, where withered corn stalks still stood upright, some just into the ditch by the road. We were all flat on our tummies, taking whatever cover was available. I thought of a friend who had followed the same route before me, and had been caught. There followed arrest, interrogation, a few days spent at a crammed police station, then release. My friend did not try again, though many others did. My ankle was throbbing. In a strange way, it was good to have a rest. I remembered my father's present at the railway station: the litre bottle of schnapps and the small dagger in its leather case, now strapped to my belt. I remembered his last words, "Should you meet trouble, one or the other might bail you out. Use it." Would it come to that? While these thoughts flashed through my mind, the noise of the approaching vehicle grew louder. The light disappeared from the wall. The armoured car was now level with me. After the bend it swivelled its lights around, obviously on the look out for refugees.

Luckily, we were too near to the source of light, which threw the beam above our heads. Then for a long, long time there was silence. No one dared to move. Would the car return, or had it gone to relieve the nearby border guards?

Slowly, one after another, we all got up. Muddy, wet and somewhat tired we continued. It was no more than a few hundred yards, before quite different lights became visible. There was a village in the distance. The barrier across the road was lifted on this side - no passport control here. We were suddenly accompanied by people holding out hot mugs of cocoa, and we were ushered into what was obviously a school building nearby. Straw filled mattresses were laid out on the floor on both sides of the schoolroom. They were waiting for us. We were safe at last.

Crossings

I am a Refugee, 1956

Vienna was full of Hungarians. It was the first port of call for 200.000 refugees, and in December 1956 you heard more Hungarian spoken on the streets than German. My uncle and I looked up an old aunt of ours. I had never met Tante Lola, but she knew my uncle. Tante Lola lived in the centre of the city, and she put us up for one night, and offered us tea with milk. It was a first for me, when I saw the milk swirling around in the tea cup changing the colour of the familiar liquid. In Hungary we only knew black tea, or tea with lemon. We discussed our situation, and agreed that there were too many refugees in Vienna, and we could not stay with her. Tante Lola knew that in Salzburg there was a large American air force base, where they also dealt with Hungarian refugees. We found out how to get there, and we were put on a bus next evening, after I had managed to send a telex back to my Mother to let her know I was all right. I had also wandered into a bank and poured onto the counter a small bagful of all kinds of coins I had collected in Hungary over the years. They were very kind. With a faint smile, they gave me Austrian schillings. It was enough to buy a couple of tins of sardines, and a few green bananas that I posted back to my Mother.

Then we got on the bus. It was to be an overnight journey - in those days there were no motorways. It was a memorable and eye-opening ride. After the War, Austria had been split into four zones. The Russians, last of the occupying forces had only left Vienna a couple of years earlier. It had taken them nine years to leave. Austria was lucky; it took much longer for many other countries.

The badly lit outskirts of Vienna were slowly left behind, and we travelled in complete darkness through villages and small towns. Ten years after the war we could still pick out the spires of burnt-out churches in the main squares of the villages as we passed – there were no by-passes in those days. As we progressed, and approached what had been the French sector, there were lights. Villages became more alive. The night was not pitch dark any more. We could see cinemas, and fascias were lit. Occasional neon lights lit up restaurants and businesses. There appeared to be life, not just darkness in the night.

In the early hours of the morning, I must have dozed off. When I opened my eyes again it was still dark, but there were illuminations everywhere. We were in the once American occupied zone. We were driving through a city ablaze with lights and life. Street lights rendered the night bright. Glaring, brightly coloured signs lit up the place. There had been no such things in post war Hungary. We only saw them in films, and those were black and white, of course. Here, the new modern buildings were illuminated to be observed, a feast for my eyes. This was Salzburg, and the city glittered. It looked like a jewel box. This was a different world.

I didn't know I would spend nearly two months here. The place was geared to get people to America, but I wanted to go to England. Although I had three aunts in Paris, half sisters of my father, I didn't like one of my aunt's negative comments, nor the reply-paid envelope from France. I had no intention of going to France. As far back as 1953, I had sneaked in to the British Embassy in Budapest to see the Coronation film. I didn't care if I had been noticed - I had no brownie points to lose. The film had not been advertised, but people had got to know about it. I was bowled over. I had seen plenty of big state-organised events in Hungary, but this was something out of this world. I wanted to live where people still believed in tradition, and all that the Coronation meant. My mind was made up. I wanted to go to England.

Tante Lola wrote about me to Mrs Roberts, a friend of hers who lived in Cardiff. She had been a refugee herself from Austria and she was willing to help this new generation of displaced people. She replied promptly, and suggested that I go to Cardiff. If possible, they would help me to enrol in the architecture course I was hankering for. But while I waited, I began to help myself.

The ex-army camp housed most of the refugees, who were efficiently dispatched to the USA after a form filling exercise. These were the only papers with which refugees could reach that promised land, the United States of America. Most of us had arrived with no ID cards, and we certainly did not have passports. When the Americans found out that I was able to fill in their numerous forms in English, German and Hungarian, I had a job. I was paid for the multilingual form-filling at American rates. I had never felt so rich in my life. My companions were soon gone, but I was no nearer getting to England.

Of course, two months of waiting is nothing compared with the years and

In Salzburg, 1956

years of waiting experienced by some of the displaced people living there in camps since the War. The admission quotas imposed by various countries kept them there. There were many such people in Salzburg, where a second generation was growing up. They looked with envy at these new arrivals who were whisked away within days. The world's attention was focused on the new refugees. The Suez crisis had taken the headlines, and the West was not keen risking another war. Hungary had been denied any kind of help, since that might have led to further confrontation with the Soviet Union. Thus the world had a guilty conscience, and therefore the refugees pouring out of a Hungary crushed again by the Soviets, received all the help the West could offer. And that help was considerable.

However, Salzburg was not very well geared for flights to Great Britain. There were only a few, and I was due to get on the last aeroplane leaving before Christmas. But the organisation was so bad that the bus carrying the group of us arrived at the airport just as the plane took off. We were left behind.

So it was Christmas in Salzburg. The city glittered like a precious stone in a velvet lined jewel box. All the shops were full of luxury goods we had only heard of. I had never seen such riches before. The window dressing, the presentation, the packaging was sheer delight to eyes used to the drab shops behind the Iron Curtain.

By courtesy of Volkmar, a very young man I had met who hoped for better things to come, I was invited by his mother to spend Christmas with them. I accepted. It was good to be with a family, rather than on my own or with a lot of other refugees.

Christmas Eve arrived, and my father contrived to put a phone call through, while I managed to have a good cry. The tree was lit - it reached to the ceiling of the living room. Gifts were exchanged. Volkmar's mother gave me a couple of bras. I had never worn a bra before. We just did not in Hungary, not my age group, anyway. So this is part and parcel of life in the West, I thought, and I put one of them on. In my new attire, we set out with some of the family to midnight mass in the cathedral. We walked along the bank of the Salsach, perhaps for a mile and a half. in crisp, fresh snow. The sky was starless, but there were lights everywhere. The night was brilliant; the cathedral was majestic with snow sitting on all its ledges, nooks and crevices glittering in the floodlights. It was like a fairy tale. The church was full. It was a long service. There was plenty of time to make a wish, which I did. I wished for a lot, like a child at a party. I am glad I did. Someone must have listened.

A few days later, having found out that there was nothing going to England for weeks, I packed my bag and went back to Vienna. I could buy my own railway ticket! I was rich - I had been paid American rates while I worked. In Vienna, I stayed in a camp where Kis Kereszt and my uncle were waiting for their transport to Brazil, to join Tomi, my cousin.

Kis Kereszt and Uncle Tibor

I also looked up Eva and Vera, my childhood twin friends, who had let me know they were in Vienna. They had followed me after my safe arrival in Austria. We sat on straw filled mattresses in a school room in Vienna discussing where we wanted to go. They had lost their father, and barely survived the Nazi horrors with their mother. They wanted to go overseas, as far as possible from Europe. I understood that, but I wanted to stay in Europe. We said another goodbye, and eventually I managed to get on a train bound for the other side of the Channel.

It was another overnight journey with many stops. At each station people handed out hot chocolate, sewing kits or washing kits to the refugees filling the train. A little girl on the opposite seat had a bad cough which I caught from her - so much so, that when I arrived in Cardiff Mrs Roberts plied me with hot milk, brandy and honey and sent me to the lung clinic. She became my sponsor, and wanted to be a surrogate mother, since she had no children of her own.

Ostend was only a name on the map for me. We reached it in daylight, and we boarded a ship to cross the Channel. We were treated to a meal at tables laid with white damask table cloths, with serviettes and flowers. I sat by a window and watched the coast basking in the winter sunshine becoming more and more remote. It is hard to describe my feelings as the shores of Europe disappeared in the distance. To the west a new life was waiting. It was exhilarating.

Channel Crossing

January 22nd, 1957.
Vienna railway station,
badly lit, and full of people
without sure destination.

We left the camps,
the crowded habitation,
having escaped
our country's devastation.

Having got this far
and escaped damnation
what do we know
of our own expectations?

II

"The train is moving!"
Up goes the exclamation.
This is no express,
 but rumbles through the stations.

In the night children cry;
monotonous conversation;
little sleep;
more frustration.

Across Europe through the night,
greeted at stations
with gifts and kindly words,
even some information

The taste of hot chocolate,
welcome restoration
warms tired spirits
at each and every station.

Dawn breaks; lights fade;
sudden transformation.
The edge of the Continent –
a half-way destination.

III

We greet the Channel, sacred stream,
with sense of veneration,
The train of refugees-
with no identification:

local dignitaries come,
combat complications.
We board the boat
with growing trepidation.

Sailing by boat, or ship,
for some, is just vacation;
for us who leave the Continent
a different sensation.

The stretch of water grows between us
tears well up with emotion
The promised land approaches-
Is this just imagination?

Called down to earth,
the smell of food starts salivation:
"Proceed to the dining room."
We find a marvellous collation.

White napkins and cut glass
full of floral decorations!
Although more camps await us,
this is a different situation.

To the East, shores fade away
We watch with growing fascination
Good-bye Europe's yesterday:
sun flames to west ward - and salvation.

Ostend to Dover, slow farewell;
four hours to feel the separation.
Profoundly moved, we meditate:
Is this start of integration?

New Beginnings

On the 22nd January, 1957, after the Channel crossing, I found myself on a train in the company of other refugees who had all travelled from Austrian camps. There was not much to see, it was getting dark. There was nothing poetic or attractive about the way we proceeded. None of us had a very clear knowledge of the geography of Great Britain, but the lights we passed must have been London. We didn't stop, the train carried on through the night to an unknown destination, at least, unknown to us. Finally, we arrived at Snowshill station in Birmingham - I had heard about Birmingham! There buses were waiting for us. There was a short drive to an army camp, where some supper, and beds made up with an army blanket were ready for us. The organisation was impressive, but it was very cold and I was freezing in my bed. Another blanket would have been welcome. I suppose we were tired as well as emotionally exhausted.

Next morning at breakfast I made the acquaintance of salted butter. I could not believe that I was supposed to spread that under marmalade. Later it was explained to me that that was how people preferred it. Tea with milk was also relatively new to most of us.

There was an office in the camp where our eventual departures were organised. Some people were met by friends or relatives, and they were immediately released. I phoned Mrs Roberts to arrange my journey. She confirmed to the authorities that I would be received. I was given some papers to state that I was a bona fide refugee, and I was granted residence. With the money I had earned in Salzburg, I was able to buy my own railway ticket. I was in a hurry, and I didn't want to wait until transport could be arranged some time in the future.

At Cardiff railway station I instantly identified the Robertses and they recognised me. I had my sports bag on my shoulder and a small, new suitcase I had bought in

Salzburg. Mrs Roberts was elegant and eloquent. Mr Roberts had a mop of pure white hair and a strange accent. I learned later it was Welsh, and for a while it became Standard English for me. We drove to their house overlooking Roath Park.

The house seemed very big to me: it was a large Victorian semi with an extra bedroom in the roof which was allocated to me. There was no central heating, but I had a gas fire in my room, and a large open fire roared in the living room on the first floor. The ground floor was a separate flat, which they let out.

Mrs Roberts announced that she knew what continentals liked to eat and then she served up smoked kippers for dinner! But she was right, I liked them. Next morning we established our relationship when we both appeared dressed accidentally alike in yellow jumpers and black skirts. Mr Roberts was a bit more difficult to get on with. He had expected somebody rather more domesticated, like one of the Austrian girls Mrs Roberts had imported, who cleaned for them. This ambitious, divorced female, who had only one thought in her head, was not quite to his liking. But he did his best to ease my path towards the Welsh School of Architecture, and towards a more permanent existence.

39, Tydraw Road

Although I was advised to take the Cambridge English course first, and start architecture in the following September, I was adamant. If at all possible, I wanted to start the five year course right away, although it was by now half way through the first year. I had wasted enough time in Hungary through no fault of mine. I was prepared to work hard, and failure in the first year; which my elders were afraid of, was not an option.

Within a week, I was among some twenty-five youngsters in their first year, and I quickly had to learn the imperial system. I also took the language class. With the help of Mr Roberts, who contacted the British Council, I received a minimal study grant from the World University Service.

Then I was introduced to Raymond. The Roberts' preliminary run down on him was that "He comes from a very good family, and he has been a good friend to us for years." I did not know then of Mrs Roberts' match-making plans. We were formally introduced at a cocktail party organised by the Robertses in their park-side house. It seemed quite sumptuous to me. I hardly knew the meaning of the expression 'cocktail party', but I found it quite pleasant, with lots of sherry flowing. The drink was new to me, too, and I quickly discovered that I preferred the sweet variety. Polite conversation followed.

"Oh yes, you've just arrived. The Robertses were telling me about you." His voice was pleasant enough, with a posh accent. "And how was your journey? Tell me about it."

How on earth could I tell a complete stranger, however knowledgeable or interested he appeared to be, of the escape route I had taken? "Well, after crossing the Channel, the train seemed to reach London, judging by the lights, but unfortunately it did not stop. We simply went on and on until we were told to get out. It was Birmingham. An old military camp was prepared to receive us. Having spent the coldest night of my life there, I telephoned Mrs Roberts that I had arrived. She wanted to send me some money to get the train, but I told her I had saved enough to buy my own ticket. I was eager to leave as soon as possible, not to spend a second night in barracks. They met me here at the station, and we recognised each other without red carnations."

He was quite happy with this, and complimented me on my English – so good, with such a charming accent! The 'charming accent' has infuriated me ever since, but I cannot get rid of it. It was too late, I was too old by the age of twenty to adjust the workings of my mouth to form the English vowels.

At the end of the party, Raymond did not leave with the other guests.

Raymond & Agnes, Mrs & Mr Roberts

"He is going to join us," Mrs Roberts informed me. "We are booked in at the Country Club for a dinner dance. We'll be leaving soon."

That was another surprise, among a few more to come. I was aware of being scrutinised at the dinner table. Women know when they are watched.

"Would you two like to dance?" asked Mr Roberts, and all four of us got up. Dancing was good. Raymond was good a dancer, easy to follow even when some of the dances were not familiar to me. When it came to the Viennese Waltz we were suddenly in our element. Then my memories of other waltzes in the arms of someone else came flooding back, and my spirits sank. Would I ever see Gabor again? Was he alive? What had happened to him?

"You are very quiet - or is it just breathless from the last dance?" Raymond led me back to the table.

As time passed by, several other invitations followed. I learnt he was an MP and had a busy solicitor's office in town, helped by Rodney, his partner, during his absences when Parliament was in session. Eventually, he even escorted me to my annual ball at the school of architecture. Tongues began to wag: gossip started. "Did you know? Raymond was at a charity do, with a foreign lady. And he was seen with her …" I had to laugh.

By this time the British Council had found a young couple, Beryl and Bob

Pippen, who wanted to offer a permanent home to a young mother with a baby, as they had a toddler themselves. Instead the British Council delivered me. The Robertses helped me to move, and after the obligatory cup of tea they left. Beryl and Bob didn't know what they were in for. With a strange accent I talked about their cat's 'moustache' and Beryl kept a straight face. She started my English education, giving me Jane Austen.

In the meantime, I enjoyed the course, and I tried to catch up on the missed months. Some of my colleagues lent me their notes, and some helped with technical English. All was going well, except that my money stopped coming in. I had no idea what had happened. We found out that the World University Service had moved to another address in London, and had lost my file. Beryl and Bob's generosity knew no bounds. I still had a roof above my head, breakfast and an evening meal. What I also needed was my fare, lunch and the odd piece of drawing equipment, in order to carry on.

The solution came in the form of 'the dirty little Greek'. I washed up in his café on Saturdays for twelve hours, and I returned home with my hair smelling of grease. But my earnings covered my expenditures. I also had to put up with his invitations to go for a drive - which I refused. In due course I was promoted to be a waitress. That was fine. I was not in the kitchen with him, and I got tips on top of my wages. About that time the World University Service found my file, and sent my backdated grant. Didn't I feel rich!

In the Easter break, Mrs Roberts had arranged work for me in London, in the YWCA. She knew a lady in the management there. I was to work in the cafeteria, and had a room in the building. There were long shifts, but afterwards, in my free time, I could discover London. I walked and walked. The YWCA was in Great Russell Street, in the centre of the city, a few steps from the British Museum. I don't even want to try to describe the sights I visited; many people have done that much better than I could. I absolutely loved the place and I felt sorry for myself that I had landed in Cardiff.

In the cafeteria, I met other Hungarians, among them Attila, a very old friend of mine. Ildi, his wife, went to the same school as me. Now she worked with an engineering firm as a tracer. We began to plot, and managed to achieve an offer from her firm for me to work there in my next summer holiday. I would stay with Ildi and Attila.

In my course, one could fail in two subjects (which were then carried to the following year) and still 'pass' the year I didn't want to fail two, but to make my life easier, I chose the subject I knew best and I didn't study physics at all. That way, for the time being I didn't have to bother with the new measurements. This would be no problem, I thought, in my second year. And so the end of year exams approached, and I stood with throbbing heart in front of the notice board to learn that I had passed my first year.

The greatest surprise was yet to come. Cardiff City Council gave me the grant they gave to every student. Because I had passed the year, they backdated it. Perhaps the Robertses had had a hand in this.

My term finished, and I was hell bent to spend the summer in London. The offer from Ildi's firm was still there, and I joined them. The office was near Victoria, and in our lunchtimes we had a whale of a time discovering as much as we possibly could. But all good things come to an end, and Attila and Ildi left for the America. Attila's mother had been born there, so they had a preferential passage. There was a short while left before term started and I had to return to Cardiff.

However, Raymond continued his pursuit, and took me out fairly regularly. Ordinary dinners I could cope with - I had things to wear, but when he invited me to the House of Commons' dining room I panicked. I was saving for a new pair of shoes; a new outfit would have been completely beyond my means. Mrs Roberts came to my rescue, sending me a very sober navy blue stripy suit of hers. I only had to buy a frilly top to be presentable. I must say, I enjoyed both the evening and the scenery from the terrace overlooking the Thames. The view of the illuminated County Hall and South Bank in the distance was quite overwhelming. I felt this was the centre of world.

For the start of my second year I had to return to Cardiff where my next surprise came in the form of a parcel. My mother had collected the blue overcoat, and kept it until an opportunity had presented itself to smuggle it out of the country. The opportunity came in the shape of Nikolaj whom I had met in Hungary, simply because I could speak German. He regularly travelled between Belgrade, Budapest and Vienna on business, and therefore my Mother and all my friends considered him a very good match. He was a perfect gentleman. After 1956 he often visited my Mother for news of me. They would have coffee together in a cosy corner, and no doubt talked about me. Mother asked him if he would consider smuggling a few things out of Hungary on one of his journeys, among them Maci, my teddy bear, a first birthday present I was always very fond of. Nicolaj very kindly picked up Maci and the blue coat, and then bravely carried

Agnes, in her blue coat, with Raymond and Elfi

Teddy and the wrap-over style, shawl-collared coat to Vienna, where he parcelled them up. They were posted to Cardiff, where I received them with considerable joy. I am afraid the coat and the admirer have long gone, but Maci, my teddy bear, my most loyal companion has survived in spite of occasional maltreatment from the next generation. I might just leave him to my grandsons to tell them the stories of long ago I cannot manage myself.

After a few more dates, Raymond invited me to a dinner dance at his County Club in St.Mellons. Mrs Roberts was very pleased with herself. She hoped that the young Hungarian refugee could be paired off with the not-so-young local MP. She and her friends thought that his 'knocking about with a foreign lady' would help both of our careers. I was flattered, but of course the age-old question what to wear was rather troubling me. My wardrobe did not contain real evening-wear. Beryl more or less dressed me, since luckily we were of a similar size, but she didn't have anything suitable for this, and I certainly could not afford to buy anything. (This was before the windfall of the grants.)

The British Council came to my aid. They had kept a register of the refugees and occasionally we were invited to their premises, where clothes donated by the public were piled up in a corner. As well as a rather old fashioned coat, I picked out a metallic blue silk or shantung outfit - what I would now call a cocktail dress. That would have to do. The skirt was all right but the waist and the bodice were big – at twenty-one, I had a 23 inch waist. The sweetheart neckline sat quite nicely on me and the short sleeves were manageable.

Beryl was clever with the needle, and she instructed me to undo certain seams in order to make new darts. Then we pinned it actually on me. I took it off with only a few scratches in the process. I had to learn to tack, and then I put it on again. We had several fittings before I was allowed to hand stitch. In spite of our efforts neither of us had too much confidence in our masterpiece. Still, nothing much could wrong as long as the dress did not fall apart. We put it to the test by showing it to Bob. He approved, and said he would happily take me to a function wearing it.

The evening went well, and we danced until quite late. Then, on the way home in his posh car, Raymond proposed to me in my posh dress. I hedged, and I am afraid I missed the opportunity to become Lady Agnes. Just as well - later on I found out he was gay. Mrs Roberts was furious.

I got through my second year, and in the summer of 1958 and I applied for work. I didn't particularly want to wash up again. I answered an advert for a

Ivan

structural engineering draughtsman's post. The Polish head of the local GKN office, a large steel manufacturing firm, accepted me and even returned the stamp with his answer. Lesek Slowikovski was a one-time refugee himself, and he wanted to help. He took a shine to me, and even introduced me to his mother. We went out several times, until my future husband appeared on the scene. Tam and I met when we were invited to dinner by an older couple, who had thought there might be some mileage in our meeting.

Winter was not quite over. It was wet and cold in Cardiff in early March on my birthday. Among the few cards I had received there was one from the States. Who on earth could that be? I knew some of my friends had landed in America, but we were not in the habit of sending birthday cards. The card was from Ivan, who had gone to the States to study. He had tracked me down by writing to my Mother back in Hungary. It was a pleasant enough surprise. I wrote to thank him for my card, and a correspondence started.

Then came a bombshell in the shape of an Interflora bouquet. He asked me to marry him and to continue my studies in America. How had I got myself into this situation? I had to wriggle out of it without hurting him. I told him that I wanted to continue studying in Cardiff, and that marriage was not on my agenda before I qualified. My course would take four more years.

I didn't quite live up to my prediction, but our correspondence lasted for 40 years.

Surprise Visit
Christmas 1958

The car stopped at the entrance of an old block of flats. My heart was in my mouth. How many letters had I written to this address over the last two and a half years, since the revolution had separated us?

At first there had been no address. Gabor had left the besieged country while I was stuck in the capital. For weeks I had no news of him. All his family knew was that he had left for the west part of the country, where they had a holiday villa and some land. That had brought tears to my eyes, remembering the passion filled holidays we had spent there not so long before.

Then I feared the worst. When he didn't communicate, it could mean that he had left the country on his own without letting me know; but I dismissed this possibility. What I feared most was that he was among the young men being rounded up and taken eastwards by the trainload – for that was the rumour circulating in town. If that was the case, I might never see him again, short of travelling to Siberia in search of him. How long could I wait?

Once in Vienna, I had found that the Red Cross offered to help refugees to unite separated family members. I asked after him. Little did I know that he was only a few miles away, in Germany, just on the other side of a big mountain. I only learned this when Gabor's letter reached me, months later, by which time I had safely arrived in England. A letter from Karlsruhe – the first of many – was forwarded by my Mother back in Hungary - but not before she was sure I had started my course of studies in Cardiff.

In his letter, Gabor explained what had happened while he was away from Budapest, and why he had no other choice but to escape. I believed him. Love is blind. However, now that both of us were at university, there was no reason why we could not meet again.

He made the first attempt. He tried to travel after the first summer holiday, during which he had had a chance to earn enough money to pay the student rail fare. But there were insurmountable administrative difficulties for people holding only travel documents and no passports.

I tried next, by which time it was Christmas 1958. I accepted an invitation from Gertrude, a German friend who was studying English in Cardiff. As she was going home for Christmas, we could travel together by student rail, via Paris, to a small village on the Swiss border. I was amazed how easily we could walk in and out of Switzerland, simply by following the road round. Crossing the border meant something quite different to me.

Festivities over, I had the offer of a lift from a family I had met in Cardiff. They would collect me from Gertrude's home and drive to Frankfurt where they lived. But on the way, I asked if we could call at an address in Karlsruhe (which was on the way.) I said I had a friend there. They were quite happy about this, and Klaus had duly found the address. I asked him to wait for a moment.

I pressed the entry phone on the front door of the building, an old block of flats. The door opened, and in the entrance hall I found the name I was looking for. There was no lift – just a rather badly lit staircase. I climbed the first flight of steps, and then I heard the familiar voice from the top landing: "Jesus Christ!"

It seemed a very long way up. Landing after landing I mounted the stairs to the top floor - a little breathless. He did not move to meet me, just stood there mesmerised. It was obvious that my arrival was completely unexpected.

"Since I've found you at home, you'd better come down and meet my friends. They gave me a lift from the South. I spent Christmas there," I told him, as he put his arms around me. "I made friends with them while they were staying in Wales, and they came a long way to fetch me from a little village on the German-Swiss border. The idea was to show me Frankfurt."

"And can you, could you … stay? Or … are you on your way?" he asked, with badly concealed excitement in his voice.

"Should I stay?" I asked, looking up at him. "I wonder what they'll think."

"Let's see what happens," he replied, as we reached the bottom of the stairs.

Once the introductions over, the couple could not fail to sense the tension in the air. I did not even have to ask for my suitcase to be unloaded, the two men saw to that.

"What are you going to do?" asked the woman. "Are we going to see you in Frankfurt?"

"Give me a day or two, please, and then I will follow you," I told my friends, hoping they would remember the brief conversations we had had about my boyfriend. I had told them that we had been separated in the upheaval of the Hungarian uprising in 1956, that one of us had landed in Germany the other in Great Britain. Now, with a student rail ticket I'd managed to travel for the first time, and I had taken this chance. They were very understanding and we arranged to meet later in Frankfurt.

Gabor had a small bed-sit back on the top floor. There was another student in the other room of the flat, and they shared the kitchen and the bathroom. Gabor put down my suitcase neatly so that it could be opened easily. How tidy, I thought, just like his hand writing. The margins of his letters were always straight, not a stroke out of order. But the letters were so few and far between, and I had needed them so desperately!

"Why do you write so seldom?" I burst out.

"I try to answer yours," he said, offering me a cup of coffee.

Conversation became more difficult. We sat on the chairs, which together with the bed and a wardrobe completed the rather sparse furnishings.

"I wrote to you as soon as I was settled here in Karlsruhe." He sounded apologetic.

"I suppose you thought I was still in Hungary. For weeks after you disappeared, I had no news of you, I believed you were rounded up and taken by the liberating forces to Siberia. So I left, while it was still possible. "

"I sent two picture postcards to you - one, when I got out, one a bit later when I knew I would stay here in Germany."

"My Mother didn't forward them until I was settled at the Welsh School of Architecture. She didn't send them to me while I was in the camp in Salzburg," I explained. "And your second card was from Berchtesgaden, the Eagle's Nest, Hitler's hideout! So near to Salzburg, yet so far! There was no way could we have met without papers or money. It could have turned out differently. I speak a bit of German but you don't speak English."

"Then last summer I was refused a visa to Britain!" he said. "They told me my father had some unsettled property business there. That must have happened before I was even born!"

"And I even needed a re-entry visa with my travel document," I said, and looked around for somewhere to put down my cup. There was his writing desk, covered with notes, books and the usual student clatter, in reasonable order. My eyes travelled to the ribbon tied to the bedstead. A feminine touch, if ever there was one.

"What on earth is that?" I asked, although I suddenly remembered some remarks about a Swedish girl he had mentioned in connection with the big motorbikes his fellow students had, though he did not. That must have hurt him. Back in Hungary he was one of the very few who had owned a motorbike. "That must have something to do with the frequency of your letters," I said, thinking rather more than that as I looked at the ribbon.

There was no reply.

"Have you nothing to say?" I could not understand, or did not want to. "Were your letters all a big lie? Or did you just write them, to keep me going?" Tears were now near to the surface.

"No, I meant everything I wrote. And I still mean it. But I can't see into the future."

"It is not to be seen. It is to be made. By us. It is up to us," I replied.

My last glimpse of him remained with me for a long, long time. What more was there to say? He stood by the train next day. We kissed and could hardly say good-bye, promising each other that there would never be another separation for so long.

Promises remained words. After the next long, unexplained gap in our correspondence, I could not bear it any longer. On a bleak day I tied all his letters with a pretty ribbon and returned them to the sender.

Married

By the summer, Beryl was expecting a second baby, and I understood that they would need my room. I was very sorry to leave, and I moved from bedsit to bedsit. To make sure I didn't rely on my frying pan alone Beryl had me back at their place at least once a week for a meal.

Two Hungarian couples befriended me, the Bukys and the Szurmays. Elisabeth and Tibor were an older couple, who had escaped from Hungary after the Second World War. Tibor was a high ranking army officer who would have been executed, had they stayed. During their darkest days as refugees in Austria, (I quote Elizabeth) "When we lost everything God gave us Baboca, our daughter." Baboca was only 11 years younger than me, and became like a younger sister. They had settled in Cardiff, and Elisabeth used to give me a hearty Hungarian meal once a week. Charles Buky was an architect, trained in Hungary. Together we tried to fathom out the intricacies of units and measurements used in structural calculations, while Lenke cooked delicious meals. They bought a dilapidated house that Charles was renovating himself, and they wanted to let rooms. I was delighted to join them, and I was amazed when they told me that the other room was going to be let to Tam, a fellow student. People did not know that we were going out quite regularly by then, but to move in under the same roof … well.

By the summer, Tam and I were planning to go to Italy in the holidays, but I had misgivings about travelling together. It just was not acceptable in the 1950s. So Tam ordered a bottle of wine, and asked me to marry him. I said yes. A few days later we were having dinner with Elisabeth and Tibor when Tam announced that he was getting married, and asked Uncle Tibor if he would be his best man. They were rather surprised, but he was very pleased to accept.

"And who are you marrying?" asked Elisabeth. I kept my eyes on my plate. Cheerful congratulations followed, and they opened a bottle of wine.

There was no question of a big wedding, we were both students, living on our grants, and whatever extra we could earn with Saturday jobs and during holidays. In those days when we wore gloves and hats it was unimaginable to get married in anything less than a suit, even if you were a penniless student. Therefore, I had to find a suitable outfit by the 27th June 1959.

The summer sales were approaching, and I noticed in a shop window a very simple, shawl collared suit. It was pale mauve, and straight-skirted, and would cost £1.00 on the first day. I have never liked queuing or getting up early in the morning. I still don't. But this was a very special occasion. So, there I was, on the day, at the crack of dawn, first one in the queue. I asked for the suit from the shop window. I knew it would fit, having previously found out its size. I was mightily pleased. But I still had no accessories. Friends came forward. Beryl had a lovely, lacy top her mother had crocheted for her a long time earlier. It fitted, and there were gloves to go with it. Matching shoes were lent to me, with heels I could hardly walk in, but they looked good.

My wedding ring was borrowed, because we had dismissed the superstition that borrowed rings bring bad luck. Perhaps we should have paid more attention to that superstition! Tam's ring was real – a new curtain ring.

Wedding Day: Bob Pippen, Agnes, Tam, Tibor Szurmay

We were married for better or worse in June 1959. It lasted for 28 stormy years. Immediately after the wedding we left for London, where Tam already had a holiday job, selling Eldorado ice cream at St Pancras Station. The firm gave me a small trolley, too, and we happily walked up and down the platforms, earning money for our honeymoon. On the last day Eldorado put a dream of a wedding ice cream gateau into our freezer.

For our honeymoon we went to Italy, Tam's dream country. He had previously enrolled at the university over there to study History of Art, hoping to complete two courses in two different countries. That had remained a dream. We were to set out in a clapped-out car owned by a friend of Tam's who had no driving licence, and also wanted to share the cost of petrol. We were to pick up a fourth person in Paris. There was one minor problem. Nobody had a valid driving licence. It was agreed that I should try to pass the driving test in the few intervening weeks. Of course, I failed, and we set out with only my provisional licence among the four of us.

The car misbehaved all the time. When the brakes failed somewhere south of Paris on a slight incline, the others told me not to use the handbrake because we would be left completely without brakes. I had had enough. I stopped the car and

Selling ice-cream on St Pancras Station
(My dress was made of old curtains)

got out, complete with rucksack. I don't know what Tam thought, but he followed me. From there on we hitch hiked. The car with its two remaining passengers expired a few hundred miles further south, and they had to abandon it.

From Marseilles we took an overnight train to Venice. Venice was magic, but so expensive that after two nights we had to leave it. So we were back to hitch hiking, now across the Apennines. We finally arrived in Rome, where Tam had loads of friends from his previous year's visits. They milled around us all the time - all being friendly, though I found it a bit too much.

However, I really enjoyed a day trip to Castel Gandolfo, the Pope's summer residence. It stands on the hill overlooking Lake Gandolfo, a lake containing sulphur which makes the water like liquid velvet. It is beautiful to bathe in, but also dangerous. Every year it claims a few victims who swim far too near to the centre. We were enjoying a good swim, not quite to the middle of the lake, when I noticed a dog lurking around our bags on the beach. Even Tam's professional front crawl back to the shore could not save our sandwiches.

Then we went to an audience with the Pope, who welcomed the gathering in at least two dozen different languages and gave his blessing.

Back in Rome we said good bye to lots of people, and had our last pizza and 'giuandui', a chocolate ice cream with marsala, which is simply delicious. Next day we started to hitch hike back to Cardiff. We had two memorable nights on the way. We spent one of them near a municipal rubbish ground. It was already dark when we put up our tent, and we didn't know why there were so many flies. The other one was near Calais, where we found ourselves in the morning in a gipsy caravan site. However, we got home safely.

Life in London

In the autumn of 1959 Tam started a year of professional practice in Cardiff's University Library. The following year, he would go on to a post graduate library course in London I became pregnant, and I consequently failed my studio work. It was a bit difficult to work over a drawing board in my condition, but I did pass all my other exams.

Lily was born in July 1960, and by then my typical refugee nightmares had stopped for good. I used to dream I was back in Hungary, and could not get out again, but being pregnant put an end to this, because I knew, even at a subconscious level, that I would never have had a child in Hungary.

After the year, Tam's place at the post graduate library school was confirmed and we had to move to London. I had to try to find a place somewhere for my final year of studies, and I was admitted to the Architectural Association School of Architecture.

We also had to find a place to live, and someone suitable to look after Lily.

Having found a ground floor flat in Gowan Avenue, Fulham, I used to walk with Lily in Bishop's Park, where we became friendly with Husker, a medium sized black dog, who was walked by a very homely, chatty lady. Lily always loved dogs. For her first birthday we had decided to take her to the toy department at Howells, in Cardiff, and let her choose a largish soft toy. As she was being wheeled along in her push-chair, we suddenly became aware of her saying "Vow-vow, vow-vow," several times. Indeed, among other things in the glass showcase at her level there was a dog. Of course we bought it for her, and I think she has it to this very day. Naturally, therefore, Lily was attracted to this new doggy friend. The black dog and the blond Lily looked rather pretty together. At that time she was barely taller than Husker, but she was certainly not afraid of him. The homely lady, who became our 'Aunty' Cox, had a son, Martin, but no daughter. She rather took to Lily, and since she lived a few doors away from the flat we had rented, she was prepared to look after Lily while I had to be in the studio.

I was very lucky to be accepted by the Architectural Association School of Architecture. Later on in my career, I only had to mention their name, and I always got the jobs. However, their standards were a lot higher than those in Cardiff. When I came to defend my diploma scheme, I failed. Alison Smithson, the architect and head of the jury, who was also the wife of a then high-flying architect, obviously did not like either me, or what I had done. She passed me, but she made such comments that she made the members of the jury feel I should not pass. Another year of hard slog awaited me. I did my design and my sketches, but Tam paid another colleague to draw it up for me. There were no women in the jury this time, and I passed with flying colours. Eventually the day arrived when I was qualified, and could also start work.

By the time I had finished my training, and went for my first interview in London, with the London County Council, I again needed something to wear. I had no interview training, experience, nor suitable clothes, but my heart was set on working there, as their architect's department was famous for its housing schemes. I could not possibly go before the London County Council in my standard student garb or in my wedding suit. I had worn that suit quite a lot, and as cheap things go, it now looked a bit threadbare. What does a young, budding architect wear?

Money was a bit easier by then, as Tam had started work a year earlier. We went shopping, even though there were no sales. A light brown worsted suit caught my eye. It had a short jacket and straight skirt, with a bit of a slit. What was more, there was a collarless top with a small flowery pattern, in the same colour as the suit. I thought it looked quite businesslike and elegant. Tam approved.

The big day came, and I tried to behave as a seasoned professional. The panel consisted of middle aged men: all of them wore suits, of course. I was not out of place, and I got the job. Ever afterwards I accredited my success to my new suit.

I enjoyed going daily to County Hall from Fulham. It meant a short ride on the tube to Westminster Bridge, then a pleasant walk across the river.

With my salary of £840 per annum, and Tam earning as well, we felt suddenly rich. We decided to visit Hungary in the summer. Tam had been back a year earlier when his father was dying, and that had been a traumatic experience. Refugees of the 1956 revolution had not started to visit the country then. Tam was monitored by the Foreign Office to see what, if anything, would happen to him. Luckily nothing did, except for the unpleasant police interview every visitor was subjected to.

This time we all went. We had no car, so we travelled by rail across Europe. From Vienna, we took the hydrofoil down the Danube, and arrived at Budapest in style. All my family were there at the quay side. This was the best part of the holiday. We saw members of our respective families and introduced each other to them.

I met my husband's family for the first time in the small town of Baja, on the southern border of Hungary, by the river Danube. The sleepy town has been the home of the Kabdebos for many generations. In the past they had been a fishing, shooting family, when they were not occupied with buying up more and more houses in some street. In the communist period they had only fishing left to them, and the children were taken to the river at a very early age to learn the skills and different methods of the art. When they had caught enough fish, they took the lot back to the house, where someone would prepare the famous Baja fish soup.

It was high summer when we arrived, and after a few days they decided that we should visit Csanàd, on a nearby island where the family had owned a large summer house before the war. It had been nationalised of course, and had become a workers' holiday accommodation, not available to the family any more. However, the Kabdebos' old caretaker, Uncle Joska, remained on the island, living in his tiny

At home with Mother and Grandmother

cottage. We were to be his guests, and he was to cook our dish. He was the cook *par excellence* as far as fish soup was concerned. By then I had learned that their version of fish soup is served in two stages. First the juice is poured over home made pasta, which is always freshly prepared, and is cut into long thin flat strips quite like Italian tagliatelle. This is followed by the actual fish.

There were lots of us: Marika, my sister-in-law, with her husband, two younger brothers-in-law, and three of us. To this day, I believe that I was more or less accepted by the tribe because I happen to love fish soup, Baja style or not.

The men folk had left at the crack of dawn for the river, to catch fish for the big meal on the island. Marika packed loads of onions, tomatoes, paprikas and chillies. When I saw several bags of flour being packed, complete with rolling pin and board, I raised my eyebrows. I couldn't quite believe what I saw. Surely, they didn't mean to make fresh pasta out there on an island, in the bushes? The previous day I had noticed a new shop nearby, selling various pastas. Surely they knew about it? I ventured to mention the subject. I should not have done so. Ready made pasta was sacrilege.

In blazing hot sunshine, we were taken to a jetty in the next village. From there, boats took us across to the island. Peter, my older brother-in-law, had his own boat and the old caretaker came over to fetch us. Some of the party just swam. I would have loved to join them, but at the time I was heavily pregnant with our second child.

On the island we unpacked, and the goodies emerged. Uncle Joska, who directed the cooking, had already set up the traditional cauldron, with a fire burning underneath it and water boiling in it. I could deal quite happily with onions, cutting up paprikás, and cleaning fish over large stones, but when dough-making started, and they tried to balance the floured pastry board on the uneven ground, I retreated to the water where the boats were moored. I simply lay down at the bottom of one of them and went to sleep

I was woken by the delicious smell of the famous soup. The scent of sizzling onions cooked in lard wafted through the air. Red paprika was added, and then fish of several different kinds. By the time they served the second course, I was fully awake and taking part – which was just as well, because fresh water fish is rather full of bones. They had also boiled the heads in the pot, claiming that these were the tastiest parts, and now they were served. Fish have no eyelashes, and I can clearly remember the eyes gazing at me from my plate.

Back in Budapest, we had to report to the police separately, and answer their numerous, unpleasant questions. We were pleased to have been, but I felt the visit was not a holiday.

At home, the shared bathroom of our rented flat began to grate on our nerves. It was time to think about a place of our own. Because Aunty, our trusted nanny, the kingpin of our existence lived a few doors away, it was imperative that we stayed within striking distance of her. We couldn't possibly look for anyone else. Aunty, her family, and Husker had become part of our family - or rather, we had become part of hers.

We had no savings, of course, so Tam went to the bank and asked for a loan. He told the bank manager that his employer, University College, had already granted him one with a view to buying a house. Then he went to the College authorities and told them the same story. The two loans were enough to pay a deposit on a small flat in Fulham. So we started to look for a flat. It didn't take very long before we found an end of terrace house for sale in Woodlawn Road. It had already been converted into two flats.

As luck would have it, Anna, our friend and trusted baby sitter, had wanted to buy something at the same time. She had grown tired of rented flats and was looking for a place of her own. My only request was to have the first floor flat, because over the years I had become quite neurotic with people walking, dancing and making music above our heads. Anna agreed. In any case, the ground floor flat was in much better condition because the owner himself lived in it. He was a do-it-yourself man, and he had created a self-contained unit on the first floor. Only the ground floor entrance was shared. It all worked out very nicely.

Once upstairs, five doors opened off the usual narrow long corridor. At the front of the house, the largest room stretched over the hall below. This became our bed-sit-cum-living room. The owner must have used up left over wall papers, because each of the four walls had a different one on it. Apart from that, it was a lovely room, more or less overlooking Fulham football ground, and beyond that we could see the sails of the boats on the river. We could nearly watch the boat race from our bay window, until a large stand was built for the football club. The original view compensated us for lack of furniture. There wasn't any money left for bookshelves, so I built in the two recesses by the chimney breast with orange boxes. It is quite amazing how adaptable these can be, and when the books were in place you could hardly see the framework. I also had my large drawing board which had come to live with us.

The next room, facing the back garden, became Lily's and eventually, the children's room. As they say, "A new house, a new baby," and in less than a year Andrea put in appearance. The room could easily accommodate a bunk bed and a cot, and I built in all sorts of storage units and a fold down desk for a play surface or for eventual homework.

Towards the back, two steps down, was the bathroom. It was a great moment when I first sat in our own bath without having to consider other tenants. Further down the corridor there was a very small room into which it was just possible to put a narrow, two foot six bed. Tam claimed the room for himself - he had to have his study! I designed shelves up to the ceiling, and a writing surface, which ran around the remaining walls. Last, but not least, at the back of the corridor was our dining room, with the kitchen beyond. Our dining table was my card table which in the past had supported my first, old fashioned drawing board. Later, as a house-warming present, we were given a large, oval mahogany table which cost 30 shillings from a second hand shop. Today, restored to its full splendour, with all the extendable bits and pieces, it is worth hundreds, I am told. The kitchen was quite reasonable, with built-in units but no cooker. I hired an electric cooker, and to my surprise, I began to be able to bake sponges which didn't collapse like the ones cooked in the very old gas cooker in our rented flat.

A flight of stairs led from the kitchen to the back garden we shared with Anna. We bought a lawn mower and we felt we had arrived. All this for £3000!

Andrea was born in November 1964. Then I stayed at home, and after the maternity leave was up I learned to manage on £4 a week for housekeeping. Happy days!

Aunty was prepared to look after Andrea when I went back to part time work. She used to pick up Lily from school, and came to meet me at the bus stop with Andrea in the push chair. The girls acquired a lovely Dorset accent from her, and she taught them all the nursery rhymes I didn't know. Once, I even blighted Andrea's early career. In Bishop's Park there were all sorts of entertainments, among them a band stand, a toddlers' green, a large pond, and a sand pit. One day a baby beauty contest was organised, and Andrea got to the finals. But the next day I missed the appointed hour for the finals!

With both of us working, we could afford a holiday somewhere other than Hungary. Tam's friend, Erno, lived in Arenzano, on the Italian seaside, with his wife and ten cats. The men were in the habit of discussing literary issues, and now they thought that a flat swap would be a good idea for a holiday. When I understood the layout of their flat, I suggested we invite my mother to come with us. She had not seen her second granddaughter yet, and Andrea was 9 months old.

It was all agreed, and we arranged transport. Tam, the girls and I, would fly from London to Milan, and there we would meet my mother at the airport terminal in town. We would spend the night in Milan, and go next day by train to Arenzano. The plans seemed good.

The day came, and Tam and I were at the airport with Andrea, and five year old Lily, checking in an hour before the flight, as was the requirement in those days. After a short visit to the duty free shops we were ready to go to the gate. However, it was announced that the flight was delayed by an hour. This was not a good omen.

Eventually we were called. We found our seats, and waited for take off. Lily had her own seat and Andrea sat on my lap. But instead of take off came another announcement, that because of a technical problem, the flight would again be delayed. We were served with drinks. It is not easy to eat or drink in an aircraft with a baby on your lap. The wait got longer and longer. Then Tam turned to me and said, "We're going home." He was worried about the technical problem, and did not want to fly at all.

At first I didn't take him seriously, but he meant it. I tried to explain to him that we could not possibly leave my Mother stranded in Milan without any information or money. Leaving Hungary, she was not allowed to have more than five pounds of foreign currency. We argued, and I suggested he could go home, but I would travel. He was probably too ashamed to accept that. He stayed.

After further delay we took off. I was so upset by then that I was sick - the baby on my lap didn't help. Luckily, a sick bag was available and there was no mess. The stewardess was most understanding, although she knew nothing about the preceding argument.

When things settled down I tried to find out if it was possible to get a message to Mother. She might have found out about our delay, but she must have felt awful in a strange city without the language or money. There were no mobile phones in those days. The crew agreed to try, though without much hope.

It was late at night when we landed. I took a taxi to the hotel while Tam went to the air terminal in search of Mother. At the hotel, I put the children to bed and waited. There was nothing else I could do. After a while there was movement, footsteps in the dark, a knock on the door and my mother appeared calm and collected as ever. Apparently, she had found out about our delayed flight and she patiently waited until one of us turned up. She fumbled in her handbag for a moment and pulled out a small airtight dish which she handed me. A goose liver; I guessed. So we had a midnight picnic, to the annoyance of our neighbours - our joy and perhaps our relief was too noisy.

The next day we travelled on to our destination. We collected the keys and picked our way around the ten cats. One of them was to have a litter while we were there and we were expected to deal with it.

I soon discovered that meat in Italy was much dearer than at home, but that chicken liver was abundant and cheap. The village was nice, the sea was near, and the sun was shining as it should. We could all walk to the Pineta, a beautifully fragrant pine forest, with an ice cream kiosk at the end. We loved the holiday, although the litter of cats was a bit of a problem.

Tam was to go home a few days earlier than the rest of us – why, I cannot remember. I asked Mother to stay on if we could arrange to change her return flight. Malev, the Hungarian airline was quite obliging and she stayed for a few more days.

I was rather apprehensive about our return journey by train. With two small children, I had to find my way to the railway station in Milan, and get on the train for an overnight journey in couchettes. Luckily the children were good as gold. Then came the Channel crossing, and the long queue to passport control. I had only two hands to manage a push chair, a suitcase and one small girl. I was at my

Agnes and Lily at Woodlawn Road

wits' end when Lily perked up as if she knew how I felt. "Mummy," she said, "I can see tables at the front. It is the end of the queue." At last we managed to get on the train, and at Victoria, Tam met us. We soon learned from him that our family had grown in our absence. He had smuggled one of the kittens into the country, feeding it with an eye dropper on the way.

We had a pleasant life in London. We worked hard and we played hard. However, for quite some time Tam had problems with sleeping and was prescribed sleeping pills. It was a long time before his depression was diagnosed. Depression in the 1960s was a taboo word, the condition was unmentionable. One day, however, he came home later than usual, and dived into the bathroom. I didn't think much of it until the next day when Aunty's husband brought me a cutting from a daily paper which reported that Tam had fallen on the tracks in front of an oncoming tube train. He had been pulled out, and there were no injuries. Afterwards he spent three weeks in hospital, and after treatment he was able to resume work again. He always denied that the 'fall' was a suicide attempt.

I had several different part-time jobs. Once, a partner in a big firm was looking for a part time architect. A one-off house was to be built for the owner of the Blackpool Pleasure Beach. The partner asked me if I had any objections in principle to such a project, considering that I had worked on social housing, and that I had come from a socialist country. I had none. And I believed then, and I believe now, that such a project comes by only once in a lifetime. I did the design for the new house, and all the detailed drawings. The existing house was to be demolished. We had a builder lined up. It was just going on site when our opportunity to go to Guyana came, and I could not supervise the works. I very much regretted it, but the excitement of going to South America was ample compensation. The firm gave me a hefty bonus on my departure and they sent a big flower arrangement to the boat for me. Years later, I had the opportunity to see the house, at the invitation of the owner, Mrs Thomson.

Lily and Andrea in the bunk bed

Three Years in Guyana

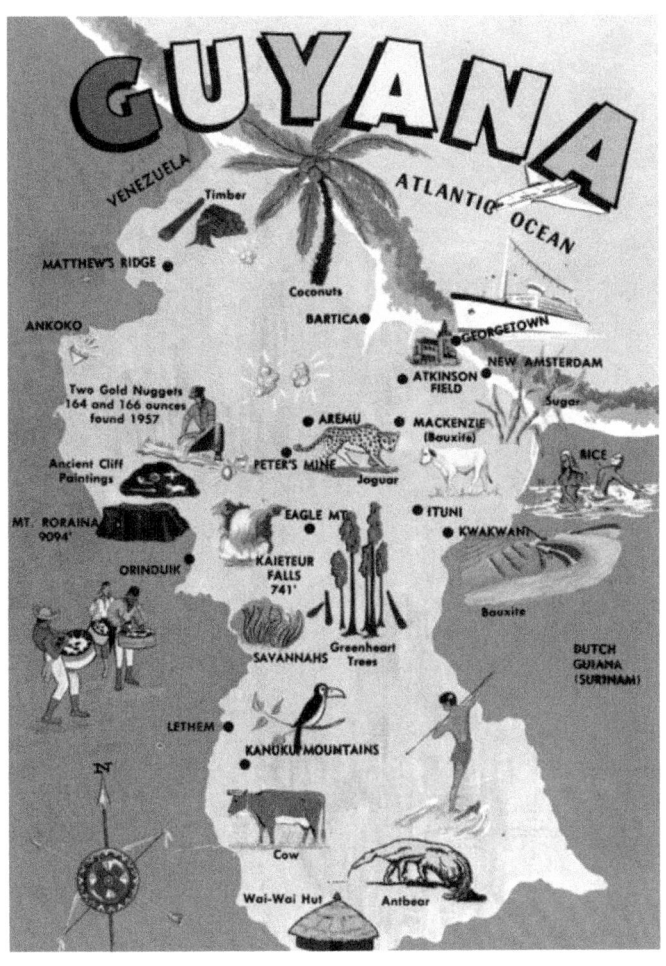

London to Georgetown

In early spring I was doing a survey of the house of the owner of the Blackpool Pleasure Beach in Garstang. Mr and Mrs Thomson were always abroad in the winter, and they returned every year to see the daffodils in their garden. The survey had to be finished by then. There was some urgency.

The housekeeper was pouring tea for us from a shiny, silver tea set. She casually mentioned that my husband had rung a little while earlier. She could not find me, and my husband had asked her to tell me that he had got the job. I would know what it was all about. I nearly dropped the china cup. It was about Guyana.

Some time earlier, Tam had started to apply for jobs abroad on a secondment basis. Addis Ababa was a possibility, but it didn't sound very appealing. My wish was to get nearer to Brazil, where my cousin and his mother, my godmother, lived.

For us, the normal fare made a visit out of the question. So I thought a posting in South America would halve the distance. Tam was equally enthusiastic. He had applied for the advertised job in ex-British Guiana, and he had his interview on the day when I was in Garstang.

Next day I returned home, and we celebrated. Tam had to take up the post to coincide with the hand–over of a new library building at the University of Guyana, in Georgetown. He was to kick-start the library, and run it for the first three years.

Guyana had been a British colony, the only one in South America, called British Guiana, up until independence in 1963. The population was 45% East Indian, 30-35% black African and the remainder Chinese and Europeans mainly of Portuguese origin. The only natives were a few Amerindian tribes. The majority of the population being Indian, it was slightly surprising that an Afro government was in power and this caused some friction between Indians and Negroes. The young people couldn't care less about the origin or colour of their classmates and friends. They mixed. Only the Chinese kept themselves to themselves and to their own when it came to marriage, though a white connection was acceptable. We were officially Brits, but our accents helped. We were very proud to have managed an equilibrium on the many occasions when we had to entertain visiting dignitaries and all races attended, instead of one or the other boycotting the event for political or racial reasons.

Tam had had to leave several months ahead of us. He flew off with one suitcase leaving me to follow with the family of two daughters and my Mother, when school had finished for Lily. She was not quite nine years old, and Andrea was in nursery school. My Mother was coming over from Hungary. I was left to arrange the move. Packing up a house three ways is not an easy task. Some of our possessions had to be got rid of, some were items we needed to take with us, and others were to go into store or to be left in the house, which we hoped to let.

I also had to finish my own work. So I was somewhat preoccupied when I drove to work during one of the last days. I turned into Fulham Palace Road on a red traffic light. A police car was behind me. The young police man cheerfully told me that he could hardly believe what he saw - that I patiently waited until the lights turned from green to red and then moved on. I apologised profusely, and he let me off! A nice farewell, I thought.

At long last, the day of our departure arrived. We were looking forward to three weeks at sea, with stops at places I could only dream of. It promised a great holiday at the expense of Tam's new employer. Our trunks had already been taken to Southampton. The car, a Ford Anglia estate, was to go with us in the hold of the boat, and we loaded it to the roof. Armed with teddy bear, toys, books and a picnic, we set off for Southampton to board the *Orange Nassau*. Friends met us at the hotel where we stayed overnight to see us off next day. I couldn't sleep all that night, the excitement was too much.

The morning passed quickly and we found the way to the docks quite easily. Our personal luggage was marked with our cabin number, and the rest stayed on the quay. We handed the car over to the boat people and then we watched with trepidation as the car was raised up in the air. The long giraffe neck of the crane slowly turned and lowered it out of our sight. We could only hope that we would see the already battered car again. After farewell hugs, kisses and tears we proceeded to a small office for a quick ticket and passport check. Then the three generations of women, my Mother, my daughters, and I were ready to climb the gangway. Apart from our handbags we only had to hold the hands of the girls

Lily and the Orange Nassau

A florist passed by with two beautiful flower arrangements.

"Those look nice. Some lucky person will have one - unless they belong to the onboard decorations," we commented.

Once on board, we were immediately escorted to our respective cabins. One had bunk beds for Lily and Andrea, and a single bed for me, my Mother was sharing in another. We had a round porthole window and the sun shone through, straight onto two bouquets on our table. They were for me. My daughters didn't understand why I burst into tears. From then on, my reputation as a probable VIP was established. I received deferential treatment from the Dutch crew for three solid weeks.

While aboard, children up to the age of ten were expected to stay in one particular area, and they were looked after by special staff. For two hours in the afternoon they were allowed on deck under parental supervision. On the other hand, the grown ups were allowed to participate in the parties, beauty contests and pancake sessions for the children. The company must have learned through bitter experience to have these regulations, both in the interest of safety, and out of consideration for other passengers.

After a bit of sea sickness across the Bay of Biscay I thoroughly enjoyed our journey. The steady hum of the engines relaxed me.

Most of the time, my Mother sat with her crochet work in a quiet corner, with panoramic view of the sea. By the time we arrived, she had nearly finished three dresses, for me and for her two granddaughters. They were made of in turquoise cotton boucle, in a sleeveless, button-through style, very suitable for the tropics. She kept me busy translating the pattern for her.

One morning as we woke up, nothing moved. The engines were still. We were docked, other boats were in view, and in front of us there was a very steep mountain covered in lush greenery and in flowers I had never seen before. We learned that this bird of paradise plant is the national flower of Madeira. We had a day trip around the island, including a sledge ride down the steep cobbled streets.

Sledge ride in Madeira

We also looked at the lovely embroidery they produce. My Mother couldn't resist reminding me of when she had tried to buy white Madeira material for a dress for me when I was about ten years old. Then, I had violently objected, I had wanted something else. Now, of course, I would be happy to have one. After tasting several glasses of madeira, we returned to the boat in high spirits.

There was a similar trip at the Azores, where the unmistakable and authentic Portuguese architecture was a surprise. Builders who had never been to Portugal managed to copy the architecture from pictures, just as they have done in Ouro Preto in Brazil, a world heritage site.

Then we crossed the Atlantic, and celebrated our entry to the Southern hemisphere. I am afraid I didn't stay up for the late night celebrations and more food, but even so I was awarded the certificate confirming that I had crossed the equator. Inside, the boat was air-conditioned and outside, on the decks there was always a breeze, so we never realised how hot and humid the weather really was, not until we docked at the mouth of the Demarera River on our arrival in Georgetown. There were only a few people to welcome the boat and I could easily pick out a figure in a pair of white shorts with a strange kind of top, neither a shirt nor a jacket, which was the fashionable garment of the newly independent country. They called it 'shirt-jack'. How sensible, given the climate! I recognised my sun-tanned husband, his arms wildly waving above the crowd. He saw us, and a wide smile spread over his face.

"Look, look! Daddy is there, waving to us," I said. It was good to see him, reassuring in the peculiar surroundings. We were given priority, and with two small daughters holding our hands, we were among the first ones on the gangway. There we breathed in the scented, warm wind which blew around us. It was a heavy, damp and slightly rotting smell. It was the atmosphere of the jungle. So this is where we are going to spend three years, I thought, though I said nothing except: "Careful, don't slip, the water looks dirty," and I tightened my grip on the girls' hands. But once ashore, the nine year old ran ahead into Daddy's arms.

We had hoped to get our car back and drive away, so we walked over to where the cars were parked. But a customs officer stopped us, and explained that the car was impounded until we paid the import tax. "Pay what?" we asked in amazement. It was a battered old Ford Anglia, and we brought it purely for our own personal use. However, there was no point in arguing with the burly, enormous chap. Tam went to find a phone to ask for help, and a colleague from the library arrived in due course to take us home. While he did this, I told the officer that I was going to remove some of our suitcases. While poking in the car I removed the rotor arm, and left the battery disconnected, just in case some unauthorised person had the idea of driving it away. A few days later, while so-called negotiations were in progress between the University and the local authorities, I asked to be taken to the compound where we had left the car. No one was around, so I replaced the missing piece, got into the car and drove away.

I thought this was the end of the story, until about a fortnight later, when I arrived home around lunchtime, and my Mother told me that three uniformed men had come and had tried to explain something to her. She was very upset. She didn't speak English, and the men spoke nothing but English – a sort of English. Finally, they simply towed our car away. This was the end of the first car we ever owned. We refused to pay the extortionate sum they demanded, and gave the car away to the University.

A few weeks after our arrival we were invited to a charity reception hosted by the London educated Prime Minister, Mr Burnham. I can't remember what he wanted to raise money for, these events were always a bit dubious. It was allegedly for some educational purpose. He elaborated on the dire economic situation of the country, and coerced the captive audience into making donations. He addressed

Agnes, Andrea and Lily in the dresses Granny crocheted on the boat.

people personally, asking how much they would offer. A representative of each bank was present in case people didn't have their chequebooks or vast amounts of cash on them. It was all very uncomfortable. The rich trading Singhs, the drinks manufacturer D'Agar, and the owners of the large Chinese supermarkets were afraid not to oblige. Then came the turn of the University, and Tam, whose name Mr Burnham couldn't pronounce, stood up, took a few steps forward, and slowly explained his family's experience with customs over the matter of our car. He ended up by saying that having donated the said car to the Library of the University of Guyana he had exhausted his finances. An embarrassed silence followed, then as one man the invited guests burst into applause. The roll call stopped. Mr Burnham just about managed to say how pleased he was with the results, and the evening ended with a glass of Guyana's national drink, a rum and ginger, for those who wanted it.

Mosquitoes

Two degrees North of the equator
in the steamy heat of tropical night
all sorts of creatures fly
practising their stinging bite.

Buzzing, swirling around your skin
looking for an opening.

Our Houses

I pinned a large map of Georgetown on the timber boarded wall of our house and after a few days I was able to navigate through town. The sea wall was the best landmark. Because Georgetown lies below sea level it was essential to build one, and the old colonial powers did it. Eighty percent of the country's population live along the narrow seashore, in the interior there are only some ranches and a few original Amerindian settlements.

During our stay we lived in two houses which were not really very different at all. Our first house in Bel Air was the last but one from the end of the road.

Our first house - A typical Guyanese house

Beyond and behind there were swampy fields. Wild tropical flowers blossomed and died within days. When I planted a common marigold seed in the garden, it came up in twenty four hours but died within a week. When the owners of the first house returned from their sabbatical leave we found another house in the next road towards the sea, in Bel Air. Here the houses were built around a small green square patch of land where the children used to ride our horse or played football.

Both houses were detached, and they were only a very short drive away from the sea. I thought we would be able to enjoy a swim in it. Little did I know! In Guyana one cao't go into the sea. The sea at Georgetown was yellow, muddy, and, strange for South America, not recommended for bathing. I had been warned but I did try, just once. My white swimsuit turned light brown in the very fine silt, and I caught a nasty ear infection. From then on we went to the creeks like everybody else.

The road leading from the sea to both of these houses was not made up it was just a dirt track with no pavements but a trench on either side, to drain the rain, when the heavens opened. Occasionally, these also provided a convenient place for the tired postman to dump his load.

The houses stood on stilts, because the ground floor was liable to flooding. Another reason was to catch as much breeze as possible, and there was, of course, more air movement higher up. Living accommodation was on the first floor, approached usually by an external flight of steps. All the walls of our first house were made of timber inside and outside. Only new, modern houses tried to imitate American construction and were built of concrete. Without air conditioning, these were like ovens. We didn't have air conditioning, or hot water for that matter, in either of the houses, and we seemed not to have any of the colds and sniffles our friends had in air conditioned homes. Cold showers, twice, sometimes three times, were the order of the day, to catch even more of the breeze all windows were louvered but we didn't have mosquito netting on them. Those little beasts found a way in, so we all slept under nets fixed to the ceiling above the beds. To tuck in the children was quite a funny procedure each night.

This house had no living space on the ground floor. The car was carefully parked between the supporting columns, clothes were dried there, and tools kept in a small store room. A wide L-shaped flight of timber stairs, roofed over but not enclosed, led to the front door. People took off their shoes on the terrace before stepping into a large open plan room. The front was furnished with seating. One would have thought that they would use light bamboo type furniture in the sticky heat but no, regular arm chairs and a settee with solid arms stood there. So we slung a hammock across the room, and it became our favourite resting place. Further back, three bedroom doors opened opposite the dining area: two of them to the side of the house and the master bedroom set apart towards the front. Simple timber partitions did not go up to the ceiling; therefore you could always hear everything. The kitchen was at the back and from a small landing stairs led down to the yard. From the landing we could watch the plot behind us being built on. Building methods were at least fifty years behind those of Europe. Little men with shovels pushed wheelbarrows full of soil to raise the ground level. When it came to pouring concrete for the supporting columns, they consolidated it by shaking the reinforcement bars, which should have been set carefully at a certain distance from the edge and left undisturbed.

The walls were painted in vivid colours, predominantly yellow, but each bedroom had its own colour. I acquired a large Indian cotton throw in bright orange with a stylised sun in the middle of it, outlined in black. We hung it on the yellow wall of the living area, and it was certainly bright and cheerful. We kept it for a long time even after our return home. It reminded us of the missing sunshine.

Our second house, Trevor and me.

Our second house, was much of the same layout, but constructed of concrete and painted pink on the outside. There was a room and washing facilities downstairs. If you had a live-in maid or servant they stayed there.

There was no garage. The car lived under the building and the drive took us to the large wrought iron gate which was kept firmly shut at all times. I often watched one of our neighbours, a local lady, who regularly stopped her car and hooted in front of her gate until the maid opened it for her. I know it was hot, but I couldn't possibly indulge in this kind of behaviour even in the 100-degree heat and 100 per cent humidity of Georgetown.

This house was a bit warmer than the traditional timber style construction, but nowhere near as bad as the single storey, bungalow type houses built on American patterns. At the side of the house a single flight of concrete steps led up to the front door. Here again one entered a large room which was divided into living and dining areas, separated by a full height timber lattic screen, which held our knick-knacks. The top of it provided my cat with a perfect vantage point from where she would grin at the dogs below. Three bedrooms and the bathroom opened from a

Interior of the house

short corridor. There was no bath, only a shower in a large tiled area, without a curtain or any kind of enclosure. The cold water was actually lukewarm, but cooled down as one went on showering. I had long arguments with friends in the physics department, because I claimed that hot water would have more cooling effect, due to evaporation on the skin surface. I never got a satisfactory explanation from them. The kitchen was also behind the screen, and a door took you to a landing and stair to the back garden. It wasn't really a garden, just a grass covered yard. Our pets and Tam's horse lived there. First thing in the morning, when I used to open the timber louvered door I would call out, "Good morning, Harry," and he, still lying down, lifted his big head, and neighed back to me.

Hot and sticky, that was Georgetown, about fifteen to twenty minutes drive from home. It was a capital full of fine wooden buildings built by the Dutch, who owned the country until 1796, when the British took over, and brought such civilising values as cricket, speaking English, and driving on the left. They also abolished slavery. The colonial houses with verandas all the way around them were the most comfortable to live in, even in our days. Those houses could breathe, and were not damp.

Good morning, Harry!

The country is a melting pot of several different cultures over several centuries. A man could be seen shoeing a horse beside a Chinese laundry across the road from the world's largest wooden cathedral. Schoolboys played cricket on the green near City Hall, and the botanical garden boasted of the world's largest water lily, the Victoria Regina. The statue of Queen Victoria which used to stand in front of the City Hall was banished here, when independence was declared. She lay on her side until a later government thought the better of it, and restored her to a vertical position.

Tree-lined roads provided shade in the city centre, and there were many different kind of trees we never had heard of, among them the lofty mora, with huge buttresses, and aerial roots stuck out above the ground, giant bromeliads, the home of golden frogs, and the greenheart, a magnificent hardwood tree of great strength used extensively in civil engineering.

Three years later after we had returned to London, Andrea, then aged eight years of age, was asked to give an account of her experiences in Guyana. This is how she saw it:

The Mora tree

When I first got to Guyana I thought it was a very nice country, but as soon as I reached the house we were going to live in, we went upstairs and it was already dark at about 6 pm when the mosquitoes were coming out.

When I first saw a mosquito I got very scared and ran into my room. But when I got in I was very startled to see a big white net hanging from the ceiling and I ran back out-side into the living room and said, 'What is that white thing in my room?' Then Daddy said 'That is a mosquito net and I said 'I hate Guyana, because of those horrid mosquitoes and this silly net.'

Then, when I went to bed that night I had an even worse surprise, I found a black beetle under my pillow and I screamed.

The school was very strict out there and it was a nun's school the name of the school was Ursuline Convent of St. Agnes. It was very nice when our family went to the Jungle where Amer-Indians lived, because we slept in hammocks and in the morning we went down to the river to swim instead of having a wash.

But in George-town another thing I didn't like about it was that about 6 pm big black beetles going for the light. Otherwise George-town was all right.

But in the middle of the day everyone went home because it was so humid, that was the worst part of the day.

Even our school broke up at 1 pm then most of us went to sleep because it was so hot. Mummy and Daddy came home for lunch then went back after having a sleep like everyone did.

In Guyana it was a custom that you ate rice with every meal.

The roads were nowhere as good as the ones in England they were full of big holes and 8 inch deep puddles which go up to a foot deep puddles, but the main roads were not so bad they were made of tar not sand and mud.

Another thing I liked about George-town was that nearly all the houses had enormous gardens that you could keep a horse, like we did and altogether we had 15 animals. We had a female dog which had puppies, then we had 3 birds, 1 horse, a turtle which we found walking across the road, 3 ducks. Our horse was very nice because every morning when we came down we said 'Good morning' and he lifted his head and neighed. It was not very far where we could ride him because there was a field about five houses away. Then our lady dog when she had puppies, *she had six of them and we kept one and we named him Bully and the lady dog's name was Kutyus. We named Bully that name because he was the first born out of the six and he bullied the others around.*

It was not very nice when we were travelling through the jungle because there were a few very big streams we had to cross which was a big difficulty because it was half mud and once we got stuck in the middle and we had to get big logs to put under the wheels so we could pull out the land rover, plus it was a six day journey to get where we wanted to get in the jungle and it was quite hard. I would not mind going back there.

Life in Guyana

Our daily routine started with a cold shower. Lily and Andrea got dressed in their freshly washed and ironed uniforms, and I felt sorry for them every day. In all that heat, they had to wear tight-waisted Peter Pan collared dresses.

We all had breakfast together before Tam saddled his horse to ride to the University at Turkeyen, a few miles away along the sea-wall. Then I had to get the girls into the car for the school run. They attended St Agnes', run by Ursuline nuns. The system was strict, old-fashioned, and the results were excellent.

My younger daughter, Andrea started school at St.Agnes'. Now she is a teacher herself, and I asked her to give me an account of the convent school as she remembers it, and to compare it, if possible, with her experience as a teacher now in England:

Our new Headmistress arrived at the school where I teach in 1994. We listened eagerly to how she would set out her policies. She told us in her first assembly that there was to be no ritual humiliation, as there had been at her school when she was a girl in Manchester. She explained that there, on Prize Day, pupils had to stand in designated places in the school hall to denote their class position. Secretly, I thought this to be a very good idea: it would cut out all the paper work and all those fiddly calculations. However, even then I knew it was politically correct to keep quiet. Not so in 1969, when I started school!

The Lady Ursuline Convent, Georgetown, Guyana, had a roomful of little chairs and tables. The Mother Superior took my mother, father and me to see this condescendingly miniature version of what I thought a school should be. I looked at my parents in dismay, surely they didn't want me to stay and play here? Sheer humiliation in my five year old eyes! However, this was to be the case. Within a week, in my ridiculous gingham dress, with its white lace collar I found myself back in the school with silly small chairs and tables.

The humiliation didn't stop here. At the end of each morning we had to sit on stone steps arranged in a very steep incline, awaiting collection by our parents. The more eager parents would be there at 12.00pm prompt. The more nonchalant ones, mine included, would stroll in at 12.30 pm with some lame excuse about the traffic! Humiliation indeed! To our five year old eyes it was a direct reflection of the esteem in which they held us.

The ritual belittling didn't stop there. Maths was on the curriculum for five year olds. Moreover homework was set too! If the weekend's sums were not done well enough, the nun in charge would write, "My, my, Andrea, Monday morning corrections" in red at the top of the page.

However, worse was yet to come. Science experiments saw us having to pour water on sand into receptacles to see what mass they held. As if we needed showing that sand was denser than water! I found it much more fun to mix the two together and enjoy playing with the gloopy mess! The nun did not see it the same way as I did. She, on the contrary, saw fit to take out a ruler from her desk and rap me sharply over the knuckles! Where was the Christian love here, I wondered many years later.

School reports from the convent were not much better: "Andrea is selfish and proud," my mother revealed to me when I was 21. Not far off the truth, I thought quietly to myself.

Twenty years later, I sit writing reports for my dear students following the school guidelines for positive feedback, 'Jade finds language lessons a challenge,' I write. School- speak for 'Jade is absolutely hopeless at languages.' I continue, 'She often loses focus in lessons.' (She is a pain in the neck and often distracts others to boot). I end hypocritically, 'If she could knuckle down to some focused work, she could, in fact, do quite well.' (If only I could get rid of her, teaching would be such a pleasure.) I sigh thoughtfully. Rounded enough, dear reader? No ritual humiliation in 2005!

In Guyana, competition was the order of the day, and once a week the best performing pupil in each form was rewarded. Some of the younger nuns ran games and went swimming with the girls. They reminded me of Maria from *The Sound of Music*.

In the meantime, Maria, our maid was left behind to make the beds, to do the cleaning and cooking. We had no washing machine, so she did a small wash every morning, while the household linen went weekly to a local laundry. Maria first learned to cook at the Amerindian village in the interior, where she was born. Whenever she went back to visit her mother, she brought back the essential spices to make the national dish, the 'pepperpot'. Later on, when she was employed by an English lady, she had learned to prepare English dishes. I taught her the rudiments of Hungarian cooking. She loved cooking, she was a natural. We ate very well.

Maria stayed with us for three years. She was honest and kind. I never had to fire her: nearly all other households did fire their maids quite regularly, after the inevitable thefts. I lost nothing while Maria was with us, except my contraceptive pills, sent to me regularly by a friendly London chemist. In the event, it was she who had become pregnant. While she was in hospital, I had a new maid, an East Indian, and this was the only time when some of my jewellery went missing. But she could make a most delicious Indian fish curry with green mangoes from our own garden. Later, we asked her to come back once a week to treat us to this dish.

Trevor and Maria

Tam went fishing regularly. When he brought home a rather large fish with teeth like a child's first teeth, Maria crossed herself and told me, "Madam, I do not touch that fish, it brings bad luck." Tam had to deal with it himself. I didn't look on while he was cleaning it but the end result which emerged from the oven was quite good. It was an oily fish, and Tam used a Hungarian recipe, baking it with lot of onions and tomatoes.

In the event, Maria lost her baby, and after she recovered, she came back to us as a live-in maid, together with her son, Trevor. He was aged between Lily and Andrea, and became part of the household. He went riding, swimming and played all the games with us and with our friend's children. Quite often I gave Trevor a lift to his school on my way to work.

I found it quite easy to get employment: there were not many architects about. Having turned down an offer from the Ministry of Works, I settled with a Guyanese-born private architect, George Henry, who had qualified in London, like me. He provided a car, and paid 'expenses', so I avoided paying the extortionate Guyanese income tax. It was all very pleasant. The office boy used to bring in cold drinks or some lunch on days when it was not my turn to take Lily and Andrea home after school, and I developed a taste for ginger beer. Usually, we all went home for lunch.

It was surprising how easily we got used to the local way of life, with a hot meal in the middle of the day and a siesta. Although officially Guyana did not observe siesta, everybody took such a long time for lunch that a short rest was possible for Tam. Then he had to return to the library, while I finished for the day. His poor horse had to be put in harness again, and they rode back to Turkeyen, where Harry spent the afternoon grazing on a loose rein tied to one of the stanchions supporting the library building, until it was time to go home again. This meant another a pleasant few miles journey for horse and rider.

However, the girls and I could have a proper siesta. In the early afternoon we didn't need nets above our beds, so my cat used to curl up next to me on Tam's vacated pillow. One day she paid me the utmost compliment. She walked into the room with head held high, and a rat dangling from her mouth. She wanted to jump up to her usual place to present it to me, and I am sure she could not understand my violent reaction. I was told this is just about the greatest compliment a cat can pay, but I was not impressed.

The afternoons were taken up by swimming or riding. Twice a week we went swimming in the pool by the sea where the children were trained. Luckily, there were a couple of lanes left for the public during these sessions, so I managed to have a dip too.

On riding afternoons, the children were left with Sergeant in the paddock. Sergeant was a jet black African, an officer from colonial days, retired from the mounted police. He ran the riding school just off the sea wall. He was a wonderful instructor. He transformed his sack of potato like pupils into riders.

Lily was soon very good, and won rosettes in the local gymkhanas. Andrea was just a lump of a little girl, and I sat with the other Mums on the seawall, talking 'orange juice', and the usual everyday domestic events of the various households. Sergeant often asked me why I didn't try it myself. "I am afraid of these big beasts," was my truthful answer. Then one afternoon I got so fed up with gossiping and orange juice talk, that I gave in, and I asked him if would take me on among the young ones. He grinned. After a couple of lessons on my own, I could join the children, and never looked back. I don't know who was more pleased, him or me. Sometimes Tam joined us at the end of the lessons, and we all had a short ride together outside the paddock. In the end we were able to ride out on our own, and deliver the invitations for my 35th birthday on horseback.

Lily won prizes at gymkhanas

When we got home we lit the mosquito coils, and we spent many evenings on our large terrace with a coil burning on either side of our chairs. After the shock of the first few weeks when the children were badly attacked by the mosquitoes, and had many infected bites, they were not bothered too much. We older ones had built up our immunity in our youth along the banks of the Danube.

There was no TV, and we relied on the radio for old BBC serials and the news. We sometimes went to the drive-in open air cinema. It was new to us to sit in our car while we watched a film. The *"Carry On"* films were then newly released, and we all had good laughs. At home, we played a lot of card games: my Mother was the master of these.

It was homework time before our evening meal. I didn't supervise what Lily and Andrea were doing. It was understood that they would come and ask whenever they felt stuck, and I took their word for homework having been done.

My Mother suffered severely from what was recognised as the European's reaction to South America. A born-and-bred city girl, she hated the fact that she couldn't walk along the streets. This was mainly because there were no made up pavements or roads in the residential neighbourhoods. In the centre there were beautiful tree lined avenues with large, old colonial houses, but it was not easy to get there, and it wasn't safe for a little old lady to walk about. I was very lucky not to be mugged in three years we were there.

My Mother couldn't speak English. We knew one Hungarian family, the Gedeons which provided her only chance to communicate with the outside world. Otherwise, she played interminable card games, and taught Lily and Andrea several of these. Eventually, she agreed that she should try to do something about learning English. So we arranged with a near neighbour, the Indian wife of one of our University contacts, to spend an hour or so every morning with my Mother to teach her English. She was an English teacher, and a very homely, big lady. But it didn't work and not surprisingly, Mother decided that she didn't want to spend three years in Guyana. She wanted to be back home for Christmas, in spite of our plans to spend Christmas in Sao Paulo with relatives. The trip was arranged, and she flew back to Hungary.

Soon after my Mother's departure, the Ministry of something or other became aware of my existence, and a work permit was refused. All good things come to an end, so did my work with George. He was taken to task for having a white ex-patriot on his staff. I had to leave.

A short period as a 'lady of leisure' followed. Playing bridge, attending coffee or charity mornings and joining bored wives, was not my idea of how to spend the next two and a half years. But it did allow me to make friends. Margo was American, and she lived nearby with her two daughters. Her husband worked in the interior, and he was a weekend visitor at home. Sometimes he didn't even turn up at the weekends. Margo was easy-going and very patient, and she taught me to play bridge. However, her patience ran out when the rumours about the reasons for her husband's infrequent home visits were confirmed. She marched into the American engineering firm's local headquarters, and explained that she might as well go home if her husband had to spend such long spells in the interior. This wasn't in their original bargain. From then on, we regularly played bridge at weekends with Margo and her husband.

My other friend, Rene, had four daughters. Sandra, her oldest was away at University in Edinburgh, Wendy and Jane were in the same school as my two daughters, and her youngest was only three years old. Sandra needed medical treatment for her knees and Rene had to return to England quite often to be with her. She usually took the youngest girl with her on these trips. In her absence, on certain days I picked up all four girls and took them home with me, until their father, Don, could come, and then we had dinner together. Don and I didn't like Guyana. We fumed about, and objected to the corrupt and degenerate management of everything. Rene was the calm one in that pair, a plump lady with a strong Scottish accent. There was peace and quiet around her. We remained life long friends.

I had to decide how to fill my time. I could learn to type, or to sew, or I could teach Rene to drive. She was often stuck for transport, but she didn't really want to drive, especially not in Guyana. Had I learned to type, I would have become my husband's private secretary for good. I didn't fancy that, I preferred to have a secretary of my own. I therefore chose to go to a Singer sewing course. It was time-consuming, and it nicely filled in my ample free time. So, of the two gadgets I had never liked, the typewriter and the sewing machine, I learned to benefit from the latter. In the end I was capable of making clothes for my growing daughters, and I even wore some of the clothes I managed to make for myself.

It was just as well, because we were short of money. Tam was on a Guyanese salary scale, which proved to be much less in reality than it had looked on paper. Don, Rene's husband, worked for the Overseas Development Agency, the ODA.

Among other things he was involved with the university, which was built and was heavily subsidised by Britain. When he learned the sort of pay Tam was on, he arranged a supplement for Tam, and a part-time lecturership for me at the Building Department. That was better than no employment at all, until the authorities again questioned my status and I had to leave.

Luckily, there was a bunch of Canadian architects putting a school building programme together for Guyana. We had met socially; they were pleased to have me, and I was more than pleased to work with them. There, at least, I was not conspicuous. What was more, they paid in Canadian dollars, straight to London. As far as the outside world was concerned, I worked again for my car and for pocket money. By the time we returned home, I was able to buy a dishwasher and a washing machine for cash. And for a while I managed to avoid the pleasures of life as a lady of leisure, and sewing.

But the school programme came to an end, and the Canadians left the country. We had nearly another year ahead of us. I was home-sick: I could have swum the ocean to be back home in London for Christmas. In Georgetown, we decorated a palm tree with home-made origami shapes to bear some resemblance to a Christmas tree. It just wasn't right. Still, for the actual Christmas celebration, we were to be with my cousin's family in Brazil. That kept me going.

In our third year in Georgetown I was approached by Norris Mitchell, another UK trained Guyanese architect, to help him out. There was a competition to design a Cultural Centre for Georgetown for the forthcoming Non-Aligned Conference of Caribbean Foreign Ministers. He wanted to submit a scheme, using his thesis design from London's Polytechnic, but it needed a bit of alteration. We submitted and won. The building had to be up and running in less than a year. We all knew that was a bit of wishful thinking.

Lo and behold, my work permit came through in record time! I made history. I went down in the embassy's records, and from then on I was always introduced as the only white British ex-patriot woman who ever held a work permit in Guyana.

Our time was up before the conference took place. Tam was offered an extension, but I wouldn't hear of it. The walls of the Cultural Centre itself were built, but it had no roof over it by the required time. An American firm was called in to cover the shell, and they produced a tent of suitable size. I was rather sorry not to have seen it.

I did, however, see how the so-called 'seaside restaurant' for the visiting dignitaries was constructed. Time was running out, and none of the local

The Benab

contractors could possibly undertake the proposed structure. To save the day, and the face of Guyana's government, the native Wai Wai Amerindians were called in to build a benab. The benab is said to be an exact replica of Wai Wai dwellings, or of the larger ones which served as a meeting place for the elders in an Amerindian settlement. It was circular in plan with a central support and timber posts all around the perimeter. The roof was thatched, and the walls were of reed or straw panels hung from the eaves. It was a very airy construction indeed. Nearly naked bodies climbed all over the roof timbers to complete the work, and the truly ethnic benab was finished in time. There was one departure from tradition, however. The Wai Wais usually put non-poisonous snakes in the thatched roof, to keep away rats, centipedes, scorpions and other pests which are attracted to the dried leaves which form the thatching. There were no snakes in the Georgetown benab.

Wai Wai's create building record for Guyana

OUR Wai Wai Indians from the far south of the Rupununi Savannahs have created a building record for Guyana. So said Mr. S.S. Ramphal, Minister of State, last Monday, as he declared open the huge benab they have constructed in Georgetown, at the head of High Street, Kingston.

The great thatched edifice, with conical roof rising 60 feet high, is built to the design of the Wai Wai's own tribal structure, unique among all Guyana's Amerindian peoples.

A stone's throw from the modern Pegasus Hotel, this outstanding construction of Guyana's indigenous people has been completed for use as a lounge at the forthcoming Conference of Non-Aligned Nations, to be held here in August. After the Conference, it is propose to preserve the structure as a national exhibit.

The benab was officially opened on Monday afternoon, by the Minister of State, in the presence of the Prime Minister, Mr. L.F.S. Burnham and the Deputy Prime Minister, Dr. Ptolemy Reid and a number of invitees. Captain Elke of the Wai Wais and some seventy of his men were present to witness the culmination of their efforts.

The great vault of the huge inverted cone-like building quite dwarfed the gathering below. The base is circular with a diameter of eighty feet. The great conical roof begins eight feet off the ground. There is no wall below that.

Mr. Ramphal congratulated the Wai Wais on creating a building record for Guyana. The benab was completed in 38 working days and will provide accommodation for 500 people.

Replying through an interpreter, the Wai Wai Captain said he and his people were thrilled to have been asked to build the benab for the International Conference. Captain Elke will be returning to Georgetown in August for the opening of the Conference as a guest of the Government.

Shopping

There is a Guyanese rhyme which goes like this:

If you eat
laba meat,
drink creek water,
you'll be back
to Guyana you'self
with your daughter.

Laba is a sort of hare-like creature whose meat is succulent, and very tasty.

There is another saying that if you throw coins into the Fontana di Trevi you will return to Rome. I deliberately did not throw any money into the fountain but I have returned ten times: I have eaten laba meat in Guyana, but I have not returned for the last 40 years. So much for sayings, superstitions and legends!

Guyana's ethnic diversity has produced an interesting range of eating options. Cheap tasty 'roties' (curry in Indian bread) are sold at Stabroek Market in Georgetown. There is a wealth of Chinese restaurants which we discovered under the guidance of our friends, Ken and Vi Lam, the Chinese owners of Guyana's best bookshop. The national dish is the 'pepperpot', an Amerindian game stew, prepared with special herbs and spices. Maria, our Amerindian maid used to bring us back some, whenever she visited her village. Mettagee was another local dish, for which the ingredients were readily available. We had a pound of salt fish ready, well soaked from the previous night. Then two large coconuts were grated and mixed well with a pint of water and squeezed through a muslin bag. We didn't wear tights in Guyana, therefore muslin bags were still in use. Once the skin and bones were removed, the fish could be put to boil in the coconut juice. Peeled plantains and other root vegetables such as eddoes, breadfruit and sweet potatoes were added. Salt beef and pork could also be put in the pot and boiled until the vegetables were tender. In the meantime, fresh dumplings were prepared and put in the pot when the vegetables were partly cooked. Sliced onions and okra were optional. I used to think that all the Guyanese vegetables were used in this dish.

Europeans mainly shopped for food in one of the two supermarkets run by Bookers and Lewis, where they bought the usual food. The owners of these supermarkets also owned large sugar plantations with pleasant club houses where we often spent our Sundays. But I liked to go to the large Stabroek market on the riverbank, with its unmistakable smell of fish and fruit. Most of the Europeans did not like to go there, they sent their maids who fitted in with the orgy of the market's colours. It was a delight to the senses, to touch, to smell and to see, although, perhaps it wasn't the cleanest possible outlet. Stalls were set out at random; there were no clear cut paths between, and you could easily get lost. There could be a fish stall next to one selling meat. In the hot sun, buckets of water were occasionally poured over the fish to keep it fresh. The water flowed everywhere, of course, and you had to pick your way through the puddles. The fish was caught first thing in the morning, although according to the smell, you would have thought otherwise. There were many kinds of fish we had never even heard of. The East Indian maid, who came once a week to cook fish curry and other Indian dishes for us, taught me which ones to buy.

Everything was cheaper, and usually very fresh on the market. Fruit was sold in abundance but not by weight. Women squatting on the ground laid out their fruit in front of them in small parcels: mangoes, guavas, oranges and lime, everything except apples. Apples didn't grow in Guyana, and Mr Burnham's government banned their import.

There were some fifty different kinds of bananas we had never seen before. Every week I bought about five pounds of sour-figs: these were small bananas, very sweet, in spite of their name, and with a little lemony tinge. They were usually sold on a branch, which added to their value in our eyes. There were never any left, we never grew tired of them in our three year stay.

European vegetables were not always available. For these we had to go to one of the supermarkets. A large Chinese shop, nearly a supermarket, offered the best

Stabroek Market

choice, but there was a sort of small holding not far from our house, where one could pick and buy local greenery. I didn't take the children to the supermarkets, but we used to go together to this place. Here they grew various vegetables, even lettuce, between water filled trenches. Andrea recalled one of these shopping trips:

We lived in an odd all-white enclave of Georgetown, Guyana. What was even odder is that we were encouraged to go to a floating vegetable garden to pick out strange looking vegetables which looked mainly like saturated spring onions. So, aged five or six, and manoeuvred by my older sister, aged nine or ten, I set off for the floating gardens, armed only with a basket and some small change.

My sister held my hand all of the way, probably subconsciously aware that if she let go of it, something disastrous would happen. It did. We wound our way across the estate of weirdly elevated houses, (they stood on stilts, as if recently landed space-beings from another planet) to an area where the houses ran out, and the road (such as it was) petered out into a dirt track. We threaded our way into the vegetable patch: a sort of patchwork garden criss-crossed by skinny little paths, which kept us apart from the mushy vegetables. I could guess what would happen if you allowed your foot to stray from the path, but while my sister held my hand I knew all would be all right.

I allowed my sister to pick out the vegetables (holding on to her hand all the while) and not looking down at the quagmire which surrounded us. Each time she bent down to choose a vegetable, a mushy squash or a floating aubergine, I adjusted my balance so as not to tip over into the un-boiled vegetable soup. By the end of the adventure I was quite pleased with myself. The basket was now full of soaking, misshapen and unmentionable vegetable matter but I had managed not to touch any of the revolting lumps! But there came the moment for which I had not calculated. My sister had to reach into her pocket to pull out the change with which to pay for the greens, and she had no free hand to hold mine (since the other hand held the basket of vegetables). I knew that impending doom was upon me. I did not even have time to finish my cry: "Lily, don't let go of my HAND!" and with a feeling of depressing inevitability I toppled over into the water. I hear you say that children of five don't experience the feeling of "depressing inevitability". I choose my words carefully. Thirty-five years later I can still recall the feeling!

My sister reached out her hand with a slightly pained and yet perplexed expression on her face. I realise now that the expression was partly due to the smell that I was emitting. I now looked and oozed as unappetising as the vegetables did! Lily did not hold my hand on the way home. I was made to walk in front of her at a safe distance, and the only human contact I had was as the maid guided me into the shower, merely touching me with her index finger at the small of my spine to prod me in. I showered fully clothed, as no-one dared to undress me. I watched with interest as the slugs and snails hit the shower tray, and wondered if they would make it down the plug hole…

My balance is much improved now, and my sister no longer needs to hold my hand, but I notice the scrapes my little son gets into each time I let go of his!

I considered it an ordeal to shop for anything else but food. To find a pair of new tyres for the car was a two day long entertainment, and finally I only got them by bribing a garage man. The same applied to clothing. I had learned to sew, and I managed reasonably well for the girls. They had uniform for school: very old-fashioned and completely unsuitable for the climate. I had offered to design a new one, and I made up a prototype of an A-line collarless dress, much easier to wear and cooler. The nuns thanked me for it, but nothing has changed. I wonder if they have the same uniform today.

For myself, I would have preferred some better fitting garments than those I could make up, or those the available dressmakers would produce. Once I accompanied Tam to a conference in Barbados, and I had the time of my life in a good department store. Bridgetown even had a Marks and Spencer's. I returned to Guyana thinking I had enough clothes for the rest of our stay. How wrong I was! In that climate clothes faded and deteriorated rather quickly. It was in the days of crimplene, and Rene once came back from a home visit with yards and yards of it. I made up dresses for all three of us and we managed to wear them. How one can get acclimatised!

The Interior and Its People

We lived in Georgetown, but we wanted to discover the country away from the normally inhabited parts. We learned that Guyana is almost the size of mainland Britain, with a population of less than a million people who live along a narrow coastal strip on the banks of the Demarera and Essequibo. The rivers are often the most practical, or indeed the only way of reaching remote settlements in the interior. They are the 'motorways' of the jungle. There are over 1000 km of navigable rivers, crossed by ferries and motor boats.

The rest of the land, more than 80%, is carpeted with equatorial forests. From the air they look like an endless green ocean, broken by the silver lines of the rivers. Much later on, there was talk of an international centre for research and conservation at Iwokrama, in the heart of the country, where the forest is about the size of Trinidad and there is an abundance of wildlife.

When we wanted to see something of the interior and its inhabitants, for instance, the St Cuthbert mission, we had to set out in a long wheelbase land rover, then transfer to a small boat with an outboard engine to reach one of the nearest Amerindian settlements. Then we followed a small river to the mission. Along the muddy banks we saw caimans. Their eyes were closed, and they lay motionless in the mud as if they were not alive. When they were captured, killed and prepared by skilled taxidermists they were for sale. Lily kept a large specimen suspended above her bed for a long time. I still have a tiny one.

We landed at the mission's jetty, and went ashore at a clearing surrounded by a huddle of timber and adobe mud brick dwellings whose floor level was always a few steps above ground. On the thatched roofs the owners placed unleavened flat breads to bake in the sunshine. Our maid Maria was a Macushi Indian, and our visit to St Cuthbert's mission, a Machusi settlement, was organised partly through her connection. We were expected. Small children gathered at a respectful distance

Amerindian School building

and watched us. Pairs of dark eyes peered from the curtains of dark straight hair. There were giggles, of course, and with a few bars of chocolate our friendship was established. Then the chief greeted us with the traditional welcome for honoured guests. He sent out youngsters to fetch coconuts. They expertly cut them into two and we were toasted with a cup of coconut milk. This we treated as our aperitif before I set up our camp stove and produced our dinner outside the rest house. We were to spend the night in this simple, open timber hut with hammocks slung from posts, criss-crossing the room. The night was cold. I woke up freezing in my hammock. There was nothing much to put on, so I collected Andrea and curled up with her in one hammock for warmth. She didn't wake up.

There were no washing facilities. The morning wash took place in the river, Amerindian style. But we also had a quick swim.

The Amerindians are gentle, hospitable people, with handsome features reflecting their Asian origin. They live by farming, hunting and fishing. Missionaries educate them there in their settlements. They have learned English, and they wear modern clothes, but traditions of mutual respect and courtesy to visitors are strong. However, education also brought the lure of town with it. Those men who are not quite satisfied with life spent with farming, hunting and fishing or the girls who don't want to spend the rest of their days preparing ingredients to make bread, or squeezing cassava for food and drink, leave the village and make for Georgetown. There they make the best employees like our maid, Maria.

We wanted to see more of the interior, of course, not just the places relatively accessible by the highways of the river. Next time we didn't take to the river, because it would have taken many days to reach Manari, not far from the Brazilian border. Instead, a small aircraft took us to a rough, makeshift airstrip.

From there a 'mini-moke', a small open land-rover type vehicle ferried us to the advertised holiday place. Towards the end of the 19th century, a Scotsman married the daughter of a local chief and established the ranch. Their descendants carried on and developed the spot into a tourist attraction, Guyana style. They built a row of rooms, not unlike American motels. Meals were served in the original building. There was electricity, supplied by their own generators, and there were bathrooms with showers.

The ranch was best known for its horses, frisky, if not quite wild sorts. When there was a gate in front of them, they didn't stop, they automatically jumped. Whenever possible they would canter so near to tree trunks that, jodhpurs or not, I thought I would be grazed by the trees. The 'vaqueros' rode them bare back, but I was frightened to death.

The owners had a constantly growing zoo, actually catching the specimens themselves. There was an anteater, a wild cat, a walrus, otters, monkeys and an anaconda, the world's biggest snake, which lived in a deep concrete pit. A colourful parrot, the scarlet macaw, was in a birdcage, and there was even a colibri; the world's smallest bird, in the collection. Children could walk among the cages to their heart's delight.

But the zoo keepers had a long way to go to capture one example of each species of Guyana's wildlife. The list of wild animal that you could see in Guyana is long. Among them is the jaguar, the largest cat in the Americas, which is seldom seen. While we were in Guyana, a mother jaguar was shot and her young cub was captured. People not far from us kept him in a cage, and we used to visit him until he grew far too big and powerful. We had thoughts of sending him to Regents Park Zoo, but it was too complicated a procedure. He was released back into the wild.

The black caiman is a cousin of the crocodile. We often saw them by the riverbanks. When we arrived by boat at a convenient beach, we used to circle a couple of times before landing. Caimans don't like the noise of the engine so they left, and we were safe to enjoy the water.

The bushmaster is a huge, lethal viper with excellent camouflage, and we never saw one. But the Amerindians could pick them out and ushered us quickly away.

The tapir is like a wild pig, the locals used to hunt and eat them. Golden frogs were tiny toxic amphibians, and there were hundreds of them. Their bigger cousins used to congregate on the concrete under our house as we approached by car. Our headlights didn't disturb them.

While we were staying on the ranch, the owners killed one of their own cows for meat. We didn't want to witness the actual slaughter so they took the animal to a clearing a short distance away. Later on we rode that way. By that time there wasn't much left of the victim, and nothing recognisable. The innards were spread around and a cloud of black vultures circled above, waiting for their turn. By next morning the spot was clean, not a shred of flesh or a drop of blood was left. The only sign of the slaughter was the trampled undergrowth, where a few blades of grass were missing. Nevertheless we enjoyed our steak that evening.

There was a creek running past the ranch, coming from the Roraima mountains. We happily swam and played in the crystal clear water. Our only discomfort was the kabura fly's bite. While we were in the water they attacked the parts of us above the water line so our shoulders suffered. You could always recognise people who spent some time in the region as all their exposed skin was covered in distinctive red blotches. The bites itch for a long time. But we never encountered a piranha, whose bite was supposed to be much more dangerous and painful.

We had the use of a boat, and we paddled long distances. The air was still as we silently glided between banks of dense foliage. The jungle formed an arch overhead, and the sun's rays barely got through. It was an experience never to forget. By the time we returned to the ranch, clouds had begun to gather. We ran to our rooms as fast as we could to dodge the kaburas. The girls and I had lightweight crepe ponchos, given to us by a friend back in London. She had been to South America before. These were an excellent present which gave the right protection. Tam just had to run faster. The mother of all storms broke that afternoon, but by next morning the sun was out, the fields were steaming and the scent in the air was intoxicating. We went down to the creek. It wasn't a creek anymore; it was a fast flowing angry river. Its banks were quite steep, some eight feet high before the storm. It flooded, and the banks had completely disappeared overnight. We didn't venture into its frothy waves.

However, we were told about another kind of frothy water, the Kaieteur falls.

At 226 metres, Kaieteur is almost five times higher than Niagara and in full flow it spews 13,000 litres per second of the Potaro River into a cloud of mist and spray. It is the counry's biggest natural attraction. Legend has it that the name of the fall commemorates Chief Kai, a chieftain of the once powerful Patamona tribe. He sacrificed himself by canoeing over the falls to appease the Great Spirit, and to save his tribe from being destroyed by a raiding party of savage Caribs. "Teur" means "falls"- hence the name Kaieteur. Folklore has it that the old man and his "wood skin" canoe were turned to stone and now form part of the rocks of Kaieteur. Perhaps he won his appeasement, for his name still marks the magical curtain of water. Of course we wanted to see it.

There were two ways of reaching it. Tam chose to rough it and went on a three day hike. The route took them through the jungle, a dark, hot, sticky place filled with things eating each other, except when they were eating the hikers. They spent the nights in hammocks, in the open, more or less awake, unable to sleep because of a choir of howler monkeys who were living up to their names, obviously wondering what tourists and travellers were doing in this largely untouched land.

Kaieteur Falls

However, Tam was very impressed with the trip, especially when the guide explained that for the natives, the jungle is a source of food, medicine, poison, musical instruments, weapons, luggage, furniture and building materials. Still, he didn't recommend it to me.

Instead, as a birthday present, he treated me to the easy option. It was a flight in a ten seater aircraft which Guyana's Air Force pilots ran on their days off.

On reaching the Potaro River above the falls our pilot gently set the aircraft down on the river between the nearly vertical cliffs which formed the gorge. I felt as if I could touch the water. We approached the lip of the falls, and suddenly the plane dropped. My stomach felt in my mouth. Some people were screaming. The pilot banked and swooped to give us the most spectacular views of the highest single drop waterfall in the world. It was a narrow, constricted stream of water cascading down to a depth we couldn't even see. When he turned back to face the falls, it felt like flying straight into the cliffs beyond. In the last possible minute he lifted the aircraft up and away.

It was a relief to land. We took a few minutes to stroll from the dirt runway to the first of several viewpoints overlooking the falls, where we could look at the tumult below. I felt dizzy. It was a gut-wrenching precipice, which didn't deter visitors from ignoring warning signs as they posed for photos on the edge of it. Back at the airport, I needed a little rest before I got behind the wheel of my car to drive back to Georgetown.

Crossing the Essequibo to Goschen House

At the beginning of our stay in Georgetown we went on trips with the University's Geology Department. These were organised with several land rovers filled with adults, children, food and petrol for the whole duration of the adventure. However, one day Tam wanted to go on our own, without children. We could stay in Goschen House, a sort of missionary rest house somewhere upriver on the Essequibo. He had been told about it by an old Amerindian who was the postman there. We could leave the children for two days with my Mother, a maid, a night watchman, and the dog. Friends with children of their own would also look in on them. We could leave no address, only a contact in Bartica: the manager of Barclays, the only bank in town who we happened to know. Off we went.

We flew by Guyana Airways to Bartica, the last port where small monoplanes could land. The sky was blue as usual and the sun scorching hot. Having walked from the airstrip to the riverside, we had to find the ferry, and the boatman who was to take us across the mile and a half of dirty-looking river. It was brown because of all the silt and mud in it. However, the boatman was not to be found, as was not unusual in Guyana, so we couldn't take the local service.

We saw a big timber yard on the river bank. Timber was floated down from places in the jungle where trees had been felled. The yard had boats, and they offered us one, which I thought very friendly of them. Of course they knew our destination on the other side of the river, so there was nothing much for them to lose. They only asked if we could row. We both knew how to row all right, having grown up on the banks of the Danube, so we thought it should be quite easy. The Danube, too, is a large river, though not quite like this one. The fact that we didn't know anything about the area, neither how fast the Essequibo was, nor whether we could find the place without the regular boatman, were hazards we chose to ignore.

Tam looked at me. His eyes were begging me to say yes. He rather liked adventures. So did I, but the thought of our children, left with my Mother back in Georgetown, troubled me.

"There is no outboard to the boat, is there?" I asked.

No, there was none to be had.

"How long will it take to row across?" I asked. It was a stupid question. It didn't really matter how long it would take for them, we were nowhere near as fit as they were.

But we set out, and rowed quite happily in the hazy, hot sunshine, both stripped to our swimsuits. We resisted the longing to take a dip in the water. We knew we had better be on our way, just in case the weather changed. In blazing sunshine, on calm waters, it was quite pleasant. We reminisced about our respective rowing careers, and we went on with nice even strokes. The river was very wide, and the gentle breeze was getting stronger. I looked anxiously up at the sky. White fluffy clouds seemed to be gathering with darkening sky in the distance. Was there going to be a storm?

It didn't take very long to get an answer. Thunder rumbled. We were not even half way. Should we turn back, or hope for the best? We didn't turn back - we just tried to row a bit faster. Soon, the sky became dark, and the wind whipped sizeable waves around us. Thunder rolled nearer, and we could see lightning. I was beginning to be afraid, but said nothing. By the time it struck all around us, I was scared stiff. How stupid and irresponsible I was! "If we ever get out of this alive I will not give in to his ideas again," I thought. "Does lightning hit water?" I could not think straight. I have never been so frightened in all my life. The thought of my children at home with my Mother did not help. The boat rocked, and I had to hold down our belongings. Tam had to go on rowing on his own. We were both tired by now. However, the other side was getting nearer. I gauged the distance; it looked as if we would not have to swim for it, after all. And it did not come to that. As fast as they had gathered, the clouds raced away and left us paddling, soaking wet, in silence. We had found nothing to say during the storm!

Although this had happened long before the days of mobile telephones, the bush telegraph must have reached the other shore ahead of us. There were people, natives from the Amerindian village, on the riverbank, waving and shouting something we did not understand. We landed at their feet amidst cheers and applause. They helped us out, took care of the boat, bags and me. It was only a short walk to Goschen House, and the end of our journey.

On our return, the postman with his motorboat towed us across the river. I noticed a piece of driftwood of a very peculiar shape. It was gently curved, nearly oval, with legs it could stand on. You could see anything in it. It reminded me of a Henry Moor sculpture. Since I could not afford the real thing, I decided to take this piece home. I grabbed it, and I knew I could just about carry it to the waiting aeroplane. Tam and the postman took our packs while I struggled behind. The aeroplane's engine was switched on while Tam held on to the retractable steps. They waited until I arrived with my log.

Some time much later, we thought we would quite like to return to Goshen house, and take the children in a somewhat less adventurous way. There was a regular boat service from Georgetown. We sailed up-river from Georgetown, starting before daybreak. This time, just before our second Christmas, there were quite a few of us. During our stay we had become friendly with a family, as people in similar circumstances do. Both husbands worked at the university, and all our children went to the same school. While I drove most of the school runs, Rene provided refreshments. We had planned this trip together. Unfortunately, however, Rene had to fly home, and took her youngest child with her. Had they been present, there would have been six daughters around, aged between six and sixteen. Our group now lacked one mother and one daughter, and we could not help overhearing loud comments on the boat, "Two husbands, five daughters and not a son, tz tz, what a woman!" We pretended not to hear, but it became a household joke.

Luckily, the weather was nice. A gentle breeze soothed the heat of the day. It was only rough where the two rivers, the Essequibo and the Demerara met the sea, and crosscurrents caused rolling. None of us was sick. The girls had started boating early in life, and we were brought up on a river. We loved everything connected with water.

As we passed the Demerara and progressed towards the Essequibo estuary, the boat started to roll. The sun came up and we could clearly see where sea and river merged. A few hours later we had reached the jetty of Parika, not far from Bartica, upriver on the other side, which we had visited on our earlier trip.

As the boat was secured to the jetty at Parika, people disembarked. Some had finished their journey, and some just wanted to get off the boat while a new crowd boarded. Few of the newcomers boarded to continue the journey, most were peddlers, selling almost everything: fruit, wild pineapples with intoxicating sweet scent, mangoes, guavas with their very strong penetrating smell, and bananas of course. And there were sweets: sticky, colourful, messy sweets, which stained the children's faces in all the colours of the rainbow.

Tam got off the boat, to bring us some food. I knew he wanted to mingle with this colourful crowd and to look around. He was off again. He was a restless man, always on the look out for new experiences, interesting, but my God, how tiring to live with! His senses were now on high alert: he wanted to absorb as much as possible: the colourful crowd, the scene, the smells, everything, to be recalled at a later date and committed to paper. He produced his books quite regularly

"If he isn't careful he will miss the boat," I thought, "and then he will have a very long walk in the sticky heat to reach us further up river at the mission." He couldn't get lost, since there was only one path along the river, soft and soggy, the vegetation ready to take over, with just a few shacks dotted along the banks. The previous time we were there, we had seen the postman pushing his ancient bike more often than using it. Not even a mountain bike would do the job. We had not envied him.

A long whistle came from the engine house, and we spotted Tam carrying an armful of freshly cooked corn on the cob. A new scent wafted towards us as he approached. The cobs were hot, beautifully fresh, wrapped in their leaves. We did not need salt, butter or whatever we normally used to have with them. Tam got a standing ovation. We all agreed, these were very much better than the goods offered by the peddlers, and we munched, quite satisfied. By the time we reached our destination we had finished them all.

Our Amerindian contacts were waiting for us, and helped to carry both luggage and children along the path to reach Goschen House. They walked barefoot, surefooted, were able to carry very heavy loads on their heads, and they were always a smiling. They did not tell us when they saw a snake, just gently guided us to walk in single file behind them. I did not have to carry anything - I just held Andrea's hand tightly, since she was the smallest of us. Sometimes we had to cross larger pools of water. Big tree trunks, cleared of their branches were thrown across them, to form bridges. Andrea was carried across these bridges by one of our helpers. The procession reminded me of a children's song:

"One little elephant balancing,
step by step on a piece of string,
thought it was such enormous fun,
that he called for another elephant to come …..

Then there were:

*"Five little elephants balancing,
step by step on a piece of string,
all of a sudden the piece of string broke
and down came all the elephant folk."*

Fortunately, we didn't. The path went on for miles and miles. It was easy on the feet: soft, though overgrown here and there. And so we came at last to our destination – the mission, and the guest house.

Our guest-house was next to the mission church, which was hidden behind dense jungle vegetation so that we didn't even notice it. When I say 'next to', I mean about quarter of a mile down-river. Up-river lived our helpers, at least half a mile away.

Here there is no need for landscape architects. It is difficult enough to clear a plot of land to build on, and the plant world is always ready to take over. The wooden guesthouse had been built on stilts, as they all are in that part of the world. When it rained, the tropical raindrops drummed on the tin roof. There were

Crossing a Log Bridge

windows, mostly with broken glass louvres and wooden shutters. It did not matter - we would have wanted them open, anyway. The large overhang of the roof kept sun and rain off the sides. All the walls were made of timber boarding. A straight flight of steps led to a covered terrace, which contained an ancient, rusty calor gas cooker, a sink and a water tap. I should mention that Guyana was the only country in South America at that time where one could safely drink tap water. A large, rough table with two sets of benches and a rocking chair completed the terrace furnishings. Two rooms opened off this terrace, and they served as bedrooms. These rooms had no ceilings, so the timber structure supporting the roof was clearly visible. Hammocks had been slung across the bedrooms, tied to the timbers, criss-crossing in odd directions around the one and only double bed, which was in a doubtful state of cleanliness.

The journey had been hot and sweaty. Having discovered the house, we decided to have a swim before we unpacked. We went down to the river, where it was even hotter and very humid, without the breeze we had felt on the terrace higher up. In spite of bathing and paddling we felt heavy. It was an effort to move at all. When we sat down in the sand, enormous red ants made a meal of us. We collected driftwood scattered around on the bank. They were rough barked, and of fantastic shapes and sizes. With a little imagination we saw shiny snakes, smooth and wet-skinned. Some branches with side shoots broken off looked like mediaeval instruments of torture.

After a while, we went back up to the house to unpack and to sort ourselves out. We unloaded. There seemed to be a lot of food. We were to spend a long weekend here, and I had planned every meal with military precision, not knowing if any fresh food would be available to us. When you are in the jungle, referred to as 'the interior', you should always have an extra meal in store. Come what may, no one ever panics on a full stomach.

Our stomachs were soon full. Even washing up can be fun under extremely primitive circumstances. None of the girls grumbled. The remaining food was carefully hung from nails, or set in water against ants.

Bedtime was fun, too. Our sleeping accommodation was sorted, and hammocks fixed. The children happily swung in them, and we were tired enough to fall instantly asleep.

Next morning we had a very strange awakening. in the filtered light of the roof rafters, I wasn't sure if I was dreaming or hallucinating. I heard "*I'm dreaming of a White Christmas"* in the unmistakable tones of Bing Crosby. Nothing could have been more incongruous. It took me a long time to figure out that it had come from the mission chapel next door where they held services. Suddenly, every hammock began to move, the children could hear it too. It was the last Sunday before Christmas.

Not quite Christmas in Guyana

A Trip to Sao Paulo

Our friends in London continuously teased us that we were on permanent holiday while we were in Guyana. This was true, but only from one point of view, and that was the weather. All year around we had the kind of climate people seek for their holidays. It was hot, but pleasant, for most of the year with an average temperature range of 24-31degrees C. On the coast the heat was tempered by sea breezes. Wet seasons which happened roughly between May and mid August and from December to the end of January were slightly cooler, at around 21C, and the natives considered it 'nippy'. The ladies wore cardigans, and the men wore hats. To be quite honest, I could not distinguish between the so-called seasons, and I badly missed the real changes from spring to summer, from autumn to winter in a temperate climate.

By the time the first Christmas approached I was homesick, so we all eagerly awaited our planned visit to Brazil to my cousin and godmother. If I had thought that to travel from Guyana to Sao Paulo would be easier and shorter than from London, I was badly mistaken. My cousin had warned me of this, and he was quite right. The actual distance is certainly less, but BOAC had a straight flight from London to Rio, and on to Sao Paulo. In South America, it meant a two days journey. From Georgetown we had to fly to Belem or to Manaus, in the north of Brazil. After an overnight stay we could go on to Rio, and change again for Sao Paulo. I went ahead with Lily and Andrea, and Tam was to follow at the end of the university term. One of our problems was that one could not buy cruseiros, because the Brazilians had a ban in force. We had met the Brazilian ambassador socially, and quite unofficially he changed some pocket money for me. I was told to take whisky or rum with me as currency, since in Manaus I would be able to change it for cash. In between the arrival of the large ships Manaus runs short of these commodities. We had plenty of whisky, and rum was a local product.

So in Manaus I set out to get some money to pay for our hotel. Luckily, a young American girl befriended us in the hotel and we had dinner together. She was willing to look after Lily and Andrea while I took myself to the docks. Manaus was a free port. It was dark by the time I walked into a small electrical shop, where I had hoped to buy a radio operated alarm clock. (This was 1969, and gadgets of this kind were quite new.) To my great relief I heard two men talking in German behind the counter. I could not have conducted my business in Portuguese. We understood each other, and one bottle of whisky bought my radio, and another two bottles were turned into cash. I was soon back in the hotel.

The night was stifling. I called the management, complaining that the air conditioning wasn't working. They assured me it was. I could not sleep in the sweaty, oppressive, steamy atmosphere, but luckily the girls were not bothered.

Next morning we went on a city tour of Manaus before we boarded our plane for Rio. We saw the opera house, a market and the Amazon, of course. To think of ladies in previous century's clothing attending a performance of opera, in that heat, left me breathless. Imagine sitting in the auditorium for hours on end, heavily corseted, and in tight-waisted dresses. No wonder they used to pass out.

From Manaus we flew for hours and hours over continuous green forest jungle as far as the eye could see. At Rio we made another change of aircraft for Sao Paulo, only an hour away. Then we flew into a storm. 'Turbulence' is too mild an expression for the bumping about and around. We saw lightning all around us, and then a voice came on: "We may have to land at another airport which is an hour and a half's drive from Sao Paulo." I had to ask neighbours to keep an eye on the girls, as I was sick, and the stewardess escorted me to the lavatory. The storm passed, or we left it behind, and we were soon heading for the right destination. On landing, I could see my cousin Tomi's familiar face in the crowd waiting for the arrivals. It was an enormous relief. The last time I had seen him was some five years earlier, in London. Now he took charge of everything and I could relax for the rest of our stay.

The last time I had seen Tomi's parents, my Godparents, was after the 1956 Hungarian revolution, when I had visited them in the refugee camp in Vienna. Some time after my visit, they had left to join Tomi in South America.

Kis Kereszt, my Godmother was sea sick all the way to South America, and she never visited Europe again. She had sent clothes to me during my student days, which fitted me perfectly. I never knew how did she managed to guess my size after the birth of the children, but she did. Now, in Sao Paulo, Kis Kereszt met Lily and Andrea for the first time, and she spoiled them as she had spoilt me a generation earlier. She has never learned to speak proper Portuguese, but she could get by on our extended shopping sprees when she added beautiful items to my very limited wardrobe. She took me to a large department store to buy dresses, and a dressmaker came to the house to fit out Lily and Andrea.

We were thoroughly spoilt. There was a maid and a cook in the household, so Celesti, Tomi's Rio born Carioca wife, would play all day with the children. She was a child at heart herself. We first met Celesti when she visited in London with Tomi. Now, as then, the years simply melted away as Tomi and I picked up the threads of our lives. I was again his youngest cousin, and Kis Kereszt continued to be my trusted aunt, as she has always been. I felt very happy and secure, and this feeling seemed to be shared by all of us. My husband Tam was quite contented after Tomi arranged for him to see some contacts in a prestigious high school run by Hungarian priests.

We were taken to their club at Morumbi to swim, to play tennis, and generally to enjoy ourselves. Tomi, a good tennis player himself, had arranged for a tennis coach called 'the Professor' to give a good start to Lily and Andrea. Even my serves improved.

There were also a few sight seeing visits. In Brazil, Sao Paulo was considered in the same way Milan is in Italy; a large, throbbing, industrial centre but on a vastly bigger scale. It is full of contrasts. In the shadow of tall luxury blocks of flats the poorest of the poor's favellas shelter on the ground. Whenever there is a storm they are likely to be washed away.

In the large City Park we sampled tea in the Japanese pavilion in Japanese style. For a few days afterwards Lily and Andrea were trying to do the same at home. The pavilion was not far from Oscar Niemeyer's renowned dome of thin reinforced concrete. Without any external finish the concrete was considered badly weathered, but in the bright light under the blue sky of the tropics it didn't seem to matter.

We also visited the Butanta, an extensive snake farm and museum. This was something quite different from any zoo or museum we had ever seen. They keep the most poisonous snakes in the open air in a deep concrete pit some 50 metres long, with vegetation at the bottom. Like snake charmers, there were a few keepers with long snakes twisted around them as, if they were talking to each other. One of them was surrounded by people, but I didn't let the children too near to him. In the museum it is explained how they extract the venom and prepare the serum from it, in the laboratories within the grounds.

On Christmas day we went to the club to wait for the arrival of Papai Noel. He arrived by helicopter, landing on a jetty in the middle of the large swimming pool, dressed in traditional robes. He must have been hot. The children's eyes were wide in amazement. They had never seen anything like this. Neither had we. Papai Noel gave a present to each and every child. It was a memorable Christmas.

Caribbean Travels

To escape the frustrations of living in Guyana, people travelled as often as they could. Expatriates and embassy staff had long home leaves. We didn't. The rich Guyanese used Trinidad as a playground, while Barbados was a bit more remote and much more expensive. Grenada was exotic, and an estate agent sold plots and villas there.

For me, Barbados was the highlight of our Caribbean travels. I accompanied Tam, who was attending a conference, and I had the time of my life. It was term time, therefore Lily and Andrea stayed in Georgetown with friends.

While Tam's conference was in session, I spent my time either in the sea, or discovering the capital, Bridgetown, a short taxi or bus ride from our hotel, the Holiday Inn. Bridgetown wasn't an overdeveloped city in those days. Built along a bay, it was airy, something in between a fishing village and an oriental bazaar. Further inland, towards the centre, were all the usual banks, administrative buildings and department stores. In a gift shop I bought a small coffee table in the shape of the map of Barbados. The legs could come off, so it was quite easy to transport. I could pack it into my suitcase and it is in my living room, in use, even today. Bridgetown also had decent department stores, and even a Marks and Spencer's.

I didn't have to shop for food in Barbados: I just enjoyed what the hotel laid on. It was great. We both liked seafood and the available spread was beyond our imagination. Long, smorgasbord type tables were laden with a great variety of fruits of the sea we had never seen before. Crabs smiled among lashings of crushed ice, prawns were playing hide and seek, scallops and strange star shaped creatures made us wonder if all this was really edible. Of course, our experience was limited to the Mediterranean, and this was Barbados in the Caribbean.

Our hotel was directly on the beach. There were advertised excursions in glass bottomed boats to see the lively underwater life. However, I simply used goggles and I snorkelled. It was fascinating; I could chase fish, nearly catching them. Some of them were goldfish. Or I could touch corals. These were cream coloured, not like the necklace my mother gave me. Hers was of a deep orange colour from the Mediterranean, and such coral was considered valuable in land-locked Hungary. I spent hours in the water, and never got tired of it. When my skin was thoroughly soaked and began to look transparent I stretched out in the sand to dry, and ordered a freshly squeezed orange juice laced with a little gin, not too much, because I soon wanted to go back into the sea. Then I reported my adventures to Tam. He was quite envious, because he had very limited free time.

Barbados University had arranged entertainments for the conference, and invited husbands and wives to these. There were open air concerts: classical chamber music in the warm tropical night sounded really strange, we had got so used to the steel band in Guyana. A formal dinner and the inevitable barbecue were both organised. Life was quite enjoyable as an accompanying spouse.

At the end of the conference we hired a car and drove around the island. We were told it was a 'must' to visit Sam Lord's Castle. The building and the grounds are probably the finest example still existing of the residence of a plantation owner in the 19th century. Sam Lord's castle was built in 1820 by Samuel Hall Lord, who was one of the most colourful characters in the history of Barbados. Legend has it that Sam used to hang lanterns on the palm trees down on the beach. Ships passing at sea saw these lights swaying gently in the breeze and would think that they had come upon a safe anchorage. They would steer for the shore, wrecking themselves in the process. The next morning, Sam's men would salvage everything they could from the wreck. While there is no conclusive evidence that Sam did engage in this type of skull-duggery, it is known that he was the sort of man who had a great attraction for women, but often treated them very badly. He beat his wife often, and locked her in the slave's dungeon. The ghost of his unhappy niece hunts the castle, which today is a luxury hotel of the highest standards. The large mirrors on the walls and some of the furniture in Sam's room are from the days he lived there.

At the height of his powers, Sam owned a great deal of plantation land on the island, but the hurricane of 1831 nearly ruined him. He ended his life much as he had lived it, under mysterious circumstances, in England at the age of 66.

We had no time or money to stay there. After having walked down the cliffs to the sea, we sampled the pool in the gorgeous grounds, and we managed to have a

Sam Lord's castle, Barbados

meal before we had to leave for the airport to fly back to Georgetown. On the way we amused ourselves by planning the next trip. We agreed it should be Grenada, the spice island, home of the nutmeg. This was going to be a family trip, including friends from the States. There were eight of us, four children and four parents. We were a jolly crowd.

There was no direct flight from Guyana, we had to fly via Trinidad and change for a smaller aircraft - a very small aircraft indeed. When we approached the island I got worried. I could not see an airport, not even an airstrip, just thick vegetation. We were flying very low, just above sea level. Then there was a rather sharp turn towards the island's mountainous edge. It looked as if we were flying straight into the rocks. The airstrip was there, and it was a short one. I wondered how often it was missed.

As we landed, a pre-arranged car picked us up. We were taken to a shop to buy basic provisions. The house where we were to stay was a short walk from the sea. Foreign developers had built a few holiday villas, and one of Tam's colleagues had bought one and let us stay there. Apart from the villas there was nothing nearby. Along the road to the sea we used to follow an old man on his donkey, selling fruit. We always bought some to quench our thirst. Finally, he gave the children a ride on his old donkey, and they never forgot him.

At our nearest beach there was a bamboo hut, a kiosk, owned and run by an ex Austrian baroness. She was now selling hot dogs and cold drinks to the visitors, under some welcome shade. She didn't tell us the story of how she got from Austria to Grenada. We would have loved to know.

On one of the more distant beaches we found a large heap of conches. The fishermen used to suck out the living animal to sell, and simply discard the shells. These were big and beautiful, and they stank. We could have them if we cared to carry the heavy items in the blazing sunshine. We took one in each hand, not having carrier bags. Back in the house we had to boil them in bleach to get rid of the smell. In the end we were rewarded with shiny, pink shells which we transported back all the way to London. Locally, they sold for a pound; in St Georges they fetched £5, and by the time they arrived in London they cost around £10. We must have saved at least £50.

One day we took a car trip around the island. We had to cross a mountain range to reach the capital, St Georges, on the other side by the sea. In spite of political instability this was a friendly place. Our two local drivers were also our guides. They were proud of their civic buildings and they even showed us their high school. There was also a memorable beach nearby. A narrow strip of land jutted out into the sea. It was not more than 20 metres wide. One side of it was covered in black volcanic sand and the other side in pure bright, white sand. This was one the main attractions of the island in the glossy travel brochures. We liked Grenada, but after a week we had to leave for Georgetown, and our friends headed back to New York.

The next family holiday, a year or so later, in 1971, was at the end of the school year. We went to Trinidad, with two other families. It was a reward trip for three eleven year olds who had all passed their exams, and, we hoped, a holiday for the parents. Margo came with her two teenage daughters. Then there were some people we had met in Guyana, the Gedeons, with son Tom and daughter Agi. While Arzen, their father, worked at the Geological Survey Unit of Guyana, Judy, his wife, used to take the children to the pool of the Tower Hotel as I took mine.

One day, not long after our arrival, I had suddenly heard a Hungarian voice calling, "Thomas, Agi, get out of the water, it is time to go home." I couldn't believe my ears. Another Hungarian family in Georgetown, Guyana! We became very friendly, and the Guyanese began to believe there are only two names in Hungary, since my husband was also called Thomas, and I am Agnes.

Now we arranged a joint holiday. In Trinidad we stayed in the hills above the hot and dusty Port of Spain, in a Benedictine monastery I had visited earlier when Tam had another conference. Then, we had been booked in the Scarlet Ibis hotel in the middle of Port of Spain, but after the first night we moved out. It was very hot, dusty, had no air-conditioning, and the whole establishment was in a doubtful state of cleanliness. We had been advised to try the Benedictine complex up in the hills where it was cooler. The Benedictines had founded a school, a seminary, a guest house and, of course, a chapel. In their workshops they trained youngsters to do woodwork. I still have some of their wooden place mats, they lasted well. The guesthouse was run by nuns. There was no luxury, only basic furnishings and a slight smell of fresh baking and disinfectant. It had been clean and welcoming. The hillside was a blaze of colour with rampant bougainvilleas, and the air smelt sweet. The nuns welcomed us as we arrived and gave us cold drinks.

During the holiday we hired cars and visited beach after beach. The sea was blue, warm and clean, and we practised our skills of limbo dancing in the sand. Margo's sixteen year old daughter always won the competitions. Then we drove back to the mountain guesthouse, where the nights were pleasantly cool.

Limbo dancing in Trinidad

One day we went to a bird sanctuary. We were taken on a trip in the swamps overgrown with all kind of reeds. Towards the end we were told to keep very quiet, because the scarlet ibises were coming home for the night. There were thousands of them. As they approached with wings spread out, the sky turned pink above us. They circled for quite some time before they settled, coming down into the trees. The branches where they perched began to look like Christmas trees, hung with scarlet decorations.

After our week we had to go back to the hot airport for our short flight back home. I was feeling depressed. On landing the stewardesses opened up, and we stepped out of the aeroplane. Warm air gushed in, blowing into our faces. It smelt heavy, damp and slightly rotting, the atmosphere of the jungle. The line of jungle trees was not far away. I looked with dismay at the ramshackle shed which was the Georgetown's airport. It could barely be called a building. I was amazed that the runway was up to the British Overseas Airways Corporation's VC10 standard, though it was the end of their South American route. So this is the place where we will spend yet another year, I thought, but I said nothing.

First, however, we had to get through immigration and customs. I had some reason to be apprehensive. In the early seventies the government of Guyana decided to ban apple import and diamond export. "Eat home produce," they said. Children are not interested in diamonds, but they do like apples. How do you explain to them that there are no apples? They kept on asking apples in spite of the juicy mangoes and highly scented guavas which we had in abundance from our garden. In Port of Spain, apples were available. I wanted a few apples for Christmas, so I decided to do something about it. We played quite a bit of tennis, and in Port of Spain I bought a box of six tennis balls. These had to be imported, as they did not grow, and were not produced in Guyana. Having broken the original seal, I replaced the balls with six suitably sized apples. Then I re-sealed the box and put it in my hand luggage. All went well until the customs officer in Georgetown asked me: "Have you brought anything back with you from abroad?"

"No, nothing," I said convincingly, and moved to lift my hand baggage off the counter top. Then a little voice chirped, "Mummy, the stones."

"Stones?" asked man of authority, and his friendly face turned rather stern.

I stopped very quickly, put the bag back on the table, and unzipped it. He looked in, obviously expecting contraband. At the bottom of the bag were the shiny pebbles which the children had collected on the beach. The relief was palpable. No one mentioned the tennis balls.

Leaving the customs office I noticed a familiar figure in the small crowd of uniformed people. Dressed in his white shorts and shirt-jack was my husband, arms waving above the crowd. He saw us, and a wide smile spread over his face. This was term time, and he had not been able to leave the library to come with us.

Parking the Pets

In 1972 the term of our contract with the University of Guyana was coming to an end. Tam was quite keen to extend our stay, but I had certainly had enough. I wanted to go home. Months and months earlier I had started to have a large travelling trunk made out of one of the most beautiful hardwoods of Guyana, the Purple Heart. I had visions of turning it into bookshelves back in London. It could not be too soon for me.

We had had no home leave during our stay, unlike people in the diplomatic service. The country was considered a tough one and it wasn't very safe either. It was just about all right during daylight, but in the evenings we kept our car windows closed, because there was very little one could do if and when a cutlass was pushed through an opening and a demand was made for money, jewellery or worse. Bully, my dog always accompanied me on the back seat of the car. The Scandinavian wife of the African Vice-chancellor of the University never went outside their home without her large alsatian dog.

When it came to packing up, it was a heart breaking task to find homes for our pets, though it was the same for everyone on a contract. The animal must have been very upset, too, being lodged in new homes every three or four years, as their owners left the country. Very few would be taken home and subjected to the six months quarantine. I decided that my cat would stay in the house. Our neighbours offered to feed her, and I thought she would eventually end up with them. She was very much 'my' cat. We had inherited her from another returning ex-pat family when they had left, and it took me several evenings to cajole her out from hiding behind the fridge. When everybody went to bed, I sat with her for hours, and placed a bowl of sweet milk on either side of the fridge in her way for when she decided to come forward. In the end she believed me.

Our dog Bully, the son of Kutyus, was born during our stay and we had kept him. Now we had to give him away. A policeman assured us that with him the dog would not be chained, according to local custom. He thought it might be possible to train Bully to be a sort of police dog. A bit late, I thought, as he was 15 months old by then. About a week later the policeman came for Bully. We all stood by his car with suspiciously shiny eyes, to wave Bully goodbye. The dog sat on the back seat, upright, rigid, the statue of concentration. He did not even look at us, he watched the road. Two days later, the policeman rang Tam in his office – since my husband would not have a phone at home – and he asked if we had seen the dog. It had disappeared. By the time Tam got home, so had the dog. He was a bit scruffy, very hungry, but happy. He told me so.

We could not very well go back on our word, and in any case, we had agreed we would not take any of our pets back with us. Therefore the whole performance had to be repeated. The policeman came, the dog sat up on the back seat and watched as intensely, if not more intensely than before. We could not say anything for a long time. There was no phone call the next day – we hoped it would all work out. Two days later the call came; the dog was lost again. Had we seen him? No, we had not, neither did he turn up at home.

Meanwhile, one Sunday, we organised a car boot sale on our drive. This was standard practice for departing families, and most of our unwanted items were sold. It was rather fun to label, price and see them off to new homes. However, it was not fun with our livestock. Kutyus, Bully's mother, was the luckiest one, she went to a farm. We had known the people for some time and she seemed to be quite happy to go with them.

A few days later it was my turn to take the children swimming. I picked up all the others, and we were on our way to the pool when Lily cried out, "Mummy, it is Bully there!" I saw a very thin, neglected sort of dog by the roadside, dragging itself along. There were many like that in Georgetown. Without hesitation I stepped on the brakes and had a better look. By that time all the children in the car were calling to him, and he understood. It was Bully. We took him home - there was no swimming that day. As I sat down after having fed him, he came to me put his head on my lap and howled. He told me in no uncertain terms, in between sobs, that he would not go back to that place, come what might, and would I please make sure no one would even try it again. I promised. In the end he saw us off, and watched the fork-lift put our travel trunk on a lorry. After our departure Bully stayed in the house with the cat. The neighbours fed them until the new tenants arrived.

I Remember……

I asked my older daughter Lily, to let me have some of her memories of our stay in Guyana. Some nicely agree, and some contrast with mine. This is how she saw life, when she was aged between nine and twelve.

I remember teaching myself to swim in the tiny seawater pool on the liner on the way over to Guyana. There my feet could not touch the ground, – unlike the pools in Fulham and Putney, so I tried to gain confidence in deep water by swimming diagonally across the corners of the pool – starting always from a wider and wider point. I always did this at times when there was nobody else in the water, so that I could not be disturbed in this endeavour, and also so that I could secretly master this skill and then appear confident in it one day when the pool was full of those who were not afraid to swim in deep water.

I remember fondly the lively games we played and competitions we were involved in during the organised children's activities on the boat, feeling privileged to sit at the adults' table occasionally at supper times,

watching them play adult card games during the day,

reading on the deck – being grateful for each day that I was not seasick,

stopping off at Madeira where we went on a fast and furious ride in a donkey cart down a long, cobbled hill, wearing the special, pointed straw hats that tourists bought there..

I remember being concerned at the pus streaming down my little sister's legs for the first few weeks in Georgetown from infected mosquito bites, made worse by her eczema, the constant bittersweet smell of sugar cane burning in the distance, and the soft, charcoal like burnt remains that used to float in through the louvres of our living room window,

my grandmother listening out for, and watching every move of our maid who lived beneath, pressing my ear to the floor of her room to see if I could hear what Eunice was saying, to find something to report to her,

ants everywhere – especially in the kitchen, where there would be regular invasions,

swarms of black beetles circling around our dining area light at night and dropping, singed, onto the table there where the whole family played cards.

I remember, the unflattering gingham blue, red and orange school uniforms we had to wear – strictly two inches below the knee – and trying to satisfy nuns by studying properly, gaining good marks and receiving the reward of being able to stand on the A marks area as opposed to the B or C area at the all important termly public 'reading of marks' at school. At school in Georgetown, my geography textbook stated that Guyana had six races. I knew representatives of them all: the Chinese Lam family who owned a large bookshop in the capital; Maria and Trevor – our Amerindian maid and her son, who was my friend and more of a brother than simply the maid's little boy, who lived in the room beneath our house in Bel Air; Rose, our tall and serene Indian maid who stood in for Maria sometimes and made fabulous fried caterpillar shaped, sugar-coated sweets for snacks; Ann Gomes, my only white native school friend of Portuguese descent, who lived a few streets away, and, as her father used to put it when I came to visit, "shone like a star at the bottom of the class"; Lorraine Semple, a large nonchalant negro classmate and bully with sores on her legs, who provoked me so much one time that I kicked them in order to avoid a fist fight – thinking I was choosing the more peaceful option, but I was still called up by Miss Fonseca the class teacher for an explanation of my behaviour. I cannot remember the sixth official race – perhaps these were the mixed race people or maybe the white colonial types from Britain and Europe like myself, or the do-gooders from North America, such as our missionary neighbours and friends the American Love family, or Sister Mildred, the Canadian head nun of the primary school I attended. In 1969, aged nine, in London, my only concept of Guyana was of a hot place with lots of black people. I felt I was supposed to have some kind of attitude towards them or opinion about them – but I could not find one. I wondered if perhaps they were frightening. Once in Guyana I still had no particular feeling about them – they were just one of the sets of darker skinned people around me. I distinguished them more by what they did not seem to do than by what they did. They did not wear saris, or as much eye catching filigree jewellery as the Indian people, and they were not as verbose as Indian people.

I remember swimming lessons at Lucknow open air pool by the sea wall in Georgetown and the kind young Canadian instructor who gave me my first real confidence in water,

the scary evening masses at the local cathedral – full of hell and damnation, refusing sometimes, therefore not to go to church even on a Sunday morning, and my father not speaking to me for weeks afterwards as punishment, thinking that somehow the nun teachers at school might also sense my crime, and trying doubly hard to impress them in lessons for this reason.

I remember working hard on getting Maxine, a very aggressive mongrel we looked after in *our first rented house to like me. He was known for growling at and biting people, and in our first few months there, had killed two of our pet chickens. About a year later, after his previous owners had returned and we had moved one street away, I felt real victory when he appeared, injured, looking for me to comfort him. I was even more impressed when, some weeks before we were due to leave Guyana, a dog whom we had kept from puppyhood found his way back to our house after we had given him away to new owners living several miles away. I could see that the kind of loyalty pets could have that I had read about in books, was real.*

I remember, horse riding. I learnt to overcome fear of being dominated by a wilful animal. A strict local police sergeant showed me techniques of controlling a horse from the ground or on its back, and he was committed to motivating me to be as impressive on horseback as a Dutch girl called Majolene – his previous prodigy - had been. He mentioned her often enough to make me want to impress him in the same way. Initially, I learnt to manoeuvre a horse in the local stable and the police paddocks. Later, the sergeant let me loose to tear around the local horse race track when it was empty. Eventually, I used to venture out alone for miles along the sea wall on horseback.

I remember loving the rainy season for its difficulties, the increased chances of snakes in the garden, the fun of having to wear wellies to come out of the house and walk to the car where the

Lily rides Trojan

149

water was nearly knee deep for children. One day a giant turtle crossed the road in front of our house during this season. Most memorable were the two trips we did for several days by jeep into the jungle, where we saw enormous metallic blue butterflies and sloths high up in the tress. We visited Amerindians in their villages, where they dried flat cassava cakes on the roofs of their mud huts, and slept in hammocks. Our convoy spent hours stuck in the mud in the middle of deserted, open savannah land when our jeeps refused to budge - sometimes, we stuffed logs before the wheels until the vehicle could move on. It did not seem worrying at the time – merely an obstacle. Although there was no sign of human life around, there seemed to be a general sense that nevertheless the next village was not that far away, and that, if necessary, help would appear from there. Even when we drove along the edge of ravines, inches away from potential disaster, it seemed simply interesting rather than dangerous.

I remember long monopoly games that continued for days with my sister, my best friend and her siblings during the summer holidays when we went to stay with her family. They had dogs that were fed on rice with a terrible smell that we referred to as 'dog rice'. It was something I could not conceive of giving to my own pets, and I was fascinated that my friend's dogs accepted it. I felt, being local dogs, they would have refused it – expecting better from non-local owners, and I was sure that if I tried this on my own dogs they would not have it for this reason.

I remember, learning about charity in Guyana. There were always beggars - mainly cripples on the streets of Georgetown, and able bodied beggars might call at our house gates daily. One time when we were driving along the main coast road, my father picked up an old Indian lady lying on the road, covered in flies, very sick, and transported her to hospital in our jeep. We were on our way home from a day of swimming, eating and sunbathing at one of the sugar cane estates frequented by colonials. She had been trying to hitchhike on the roadside to get help to live. Years later, we also transported our best friend's mother down the same road to hospital. She was in the dangerous stages of jaundice following years of excess alcohol consumption. She had not wanted to leave her home in another town, but my parents had insisted – and saved her life at that time.

I remember, live steel band music at parties, and at night, and reggae on the radio always. I had no more piano lessons while in Guyana. I could only resume those on my return to England. Possibly, as a replacement I worked on a feeling I had to dance in a free way, for which I once won money at a children's party. I was intrigued by my little sister's love of ballet lessons, but had no interest in doing this myself – preferring even to practise walking on rolling oil drums in the yard of her ballet school while waiting for her lessons to finish.

Yes, I remember Guyana.

Sailing Home

We returned by the same boat we had sailed in from Southampton three years earlier, and this was the last voyage of the Dutch boat, the *Orange Nassau,* before its retirement. There was mayhem at the loading bay, horns blowing, cranes stretching their long necks, supervisors whistling. Finally we mounted the gangway: once boarded we had quite a few drinks to celebrate our departure. Until the last moment I was expecting the arrival of some official to query my income tax return, and stop me leaving the country.

Once we were safely settled on deck, the memories of our stay flashed through my mind, both good ones and bad ones. Life was cheap in Guyana and the cutlasses were sharp. And that same cutlass might be used to cut grass. We asked a man to come back and do it again the next week, but he didn't, until the money ran out. Bananas grew on the street trees, mangoes were cheap, you could sleep under the stars. Why work?

I didn't like the need to put food in the fridge raised on a bowl filled with water where the ants would drown before reaching their target, or the need to have the dog at the back of the car when I drove on my own in the evening. I didn't feel at ease to belong to the elite, a large fish in a dirty little pond. For me, it is much more comfortable to be a medium-sized fish in a clear lake. Our three years were very interesting: unforgettable, but I would not call them enjoyable. This was all over now. The ship left the docks and headed for the open seas.

We were to call at several islands. Curacao in the Netherland Antilles was the first stop in the blue Caribbean. The island was obviously rich. Large drums of the oil refinery dominated the skyline. The houses were solidly built, and had unmistakable Dutch gabled roofs. I decided to venture out on my own because I wanted to buy some clothes for Tam, who kept on wearing his not so white tennis gear, although there were no tennis courts on the ship. I returned with a slightly patterned pair of shorts and a matching shirt, and I was very pleased with myself, until Tam announced he was not going to wear such things, and I might as well take them back. I did. With less than an hour before sailing, I was in a hurry. The shop was prepared to let me have something else, but no refund. I managed to acquire a new dress, but I almost missed the boat.

Aruba was our next port of call. We were taken to the Casibari gardens. There, amongst large rocks in the wind the "divi-divi" tree's trunk bent forty five degrees in the prevailing wind, and its crown canti-levered precariously even further.

We had a day to enjoy the blue sea, which was nicer than the small pool on the ship. Then we crossed the Caribbean Sea to Jamaica. There, we had to delay our arrival as it would have coincided with their Independence Day, and the Dutch company felt safer not to be in the docks amidst the celebrations in Kingston. The following day the town was empty, and we had a chance to discover the Blue Mountains which are as blue as the Blue Danube, i.e. they are not blue at all. They

The divi-divi tree

seemed to be near, when we saw them from the docks, but they were not. It took several hours driving on the not too good Jamaican roads to reach them, stretched out in the middle of the island along its length.

Next, the Atlantic crossing was ahead of us, and the ship made certain to provide us with all kinds of entertainment. I won a foldable waste paper basket by playing table tennis. There was also a bridge tournament. We had played throughout our stay in Georgetown, but husband and wife rarely make a good team in the amateur world. However, we were quite friendly with a young couple from the consulate who were also going home, (travelling first class of course, with en suite bathroom, while we were cooped up in a cabin with two bunk beds for the four of us and a bathroom down at the end of the corridor). Jean and I had never played together before, but we decided to enter the game as partners. Our husbands didn't give us a chance, they were not pleased that we wanted to play without them. They entered themselves Jean and I became runners up and they were even less pleased when they finished at the bottom of the pile.

Punta Delgada Azores

While crossing the Atlantic we saw many flying fish alongside the boat, and sea gulls followed us a long way. The crew faithfully made announcements every time there was something to be seen on either side of the boat, and we faithfully rushed from port to starboard. Surprisingly the boat didn't tilt.

Our last stop was at the Azores, where the architecture is predominantly Portuguese. The three white and grey arches of the City Gates in Ponte Delgada heralded Europe. After that, mainland Europe beckoned, and we soon entered the Channel. I was up at the crack of dawn, hoping to see the white cliffs of Dover in the distance. Then, with great relief, I knew we were on familiar waters, and nearly home.

Back to London

A Short Detour

Our voyage ended in Amsterdam, without calling in England. Homecoming had to wait a little longer.

When we had approached Amsterdam, the *Orange Nassau* had a tremendous reception on this, her last voyage. Hundreds of people lined the banks singing songs, playing trumpets, hooting and cheering. Amidst the noisy rattle, all formalities were completed in record time. The fruit of our three year's savings, a VW Variant, was waiting for us in the docks. It was one of those duty free transactions, not one of the larger cars on the market, but it was our first and last new car. We had planned a long continental tour including Hungary before going home. We wanted to see our families.

As our luggage was taken off the boat we loaded it ourselves into the car. It was certainly full, with two children and all our belongings, although the hold luggage was sent straight back to London. When we set out, the car was packed to the brim, and as we went on travelling, it got even worse. In the end there was considerable disorder. At the beginning of our journey I prided myself that I was able to answer questions from the girls, such as:

"Mummy, where is my cayman? We didn't leave it in Guyana, did we?"

"No, it is with us in that bag at the back."

Or from Tam:

"Do you think you could find a bottle of wine before we pitch our tent, to celebrate our umpteenth border crossing?" and I would find the wine. By the end of the journey this was impossible.

Then we set off to drive the eight hundred kilometres to Vienna. We had to observe the speed restriction for the running in period - not a comfortable way of travel on German autobahns where they have no speed limits, and where all of them are in a hurry all the time.

Lily's Cayman

It was well past midnight when we arrived in Vienna, and we had to ask a taxi to guide us to our chosen hotel. The taxi driver did not accept anything for the run. There we found Tam's sister, and his aunt who were waiting for us.

Then and there, in the middle of the night, they told me that my father had had a heart attack. He was not in danger, they said. I was horrified. He was not in danger of what? What exactly did they mean? I began to fear the inevitable loss. Would he die in Budapest while I was in Vienna? How much time would we have together? There were no answers to the questions in my head during that sleepless night.

Next day, the car had its first service, while Tam and I went to the Hungarian consulate to pick up our visas. Tam's was refused. He must have offended the sensibilities of the regime with some of his writing in the émigré press. Our plans had to be slightly changed, and we parted company. Tam had planned to see the Munich Olympics, so he just went a bit earlier. We set off to see my father.

By this time I was very worried, and was also suffering from my sleepless night. How bad was the attack? What was it they were not telling me? The questions in my mind were racing faster than the milometer. I was giving my husband's relatives a lift back to Budapest, and their presence jarred on me. This didn't make the journey easier.

Twelve year old Lily was my navigator, and she did extremely well through the narrow streets of Vienna, but I was impatient, and in a hurry. Still, I thought I'd better watch the road, or we might not arrive at all.

Luckily, there was no hold up at the border. The officials didn't exercise their usual cumbersome methods of searching the crowded vehicle. We were soon on the main road to Budapest, which was not quite a dual carriageway. And I pushed it. People in cars coming from the opposite direction shook their fists at me. They didn't like to meet someone even more aggressive than themselves. Would I get there in time? No one had referred to any urgency, but the thought would not leave me.

Eventually we arrived in Budapest. I dropped my passengers, and sped towards the well known address. I stopped in front of the big old block of flats, my pulse rate racing. There were three flights of steps yet ahead of us. The lift, of course didn't work, neither did I have had the patience to wait for it. The girls were quick, they thought all those steps to the third floor were rather fun. Then they raced around the open corridor to the far corner of the inner courtyard, and the front door of the flat. The windows and balcony of the flat overlooked a side street, so my father could not have seen us arriving, but the doorbell had hardly stopped ringing as the door was opened.

There was nothing to say. Without words we embraced, both of us trying unsuccessfully, to hold back tears of joy. Then we went with him to meet my Mother, my grandparents, and the aunts and uncles who were anxiously waiting for us. We had not seen them for three years. With a growing family, that is a long time. After the excitement of the family reunion, Father suggested dinner at a nearby restaurant. There were quite a few of us, and no single relative could have catered for so many, but they all wanted to be with us, so this seemed a good idea. We drove to the restaurant place - where I soon found out that I had locked the only remaining key to the car inside it. The other key was with Tam, who was on his way to Munich. My father came to the rescue. The small triangular front window was not completely shut, and he managed to ease it open. Sometimes it pays to be negligent. With clever fingers, and a spanner he managed to reach the door handle.

This was his introduction to the new, orange coloured vehicle. He had always had a car, but never a new one.

After our meal I had hardly settled down with the girls in my Mother's flat, in the same old building where I grew up, when the phone rang. It was my father. Tam had just rung from Munich, to let us know about the attack on the Israeli team. He did not want us to follow him, as originally planned. We should wait until the situation became clearer. He would phone in due course. Out of the frying pan and into the fire yet again! After a few days he gave the all clear, and I drove with the girls to Munich. We admired the new sports stadium, and the orderliness of a German town.

Tam felt he had to see Rome again before we could turn our noses homeward. We were quite regular visitors. Lily was christened in St Peter's and by 1972 I had visited Rome about eight times. Tam was in love with the place. I, on the other hand, could hardly wait to get home. We went to Rome.

We stayed in the house of St. Steven: it was named after Hungary's first king.

The VW Variant

This was the place the Catholic Church established after the Second World War for Hungarian visitors arriving from East or West, well before the fall of the Berlin wall. The large flat in an Italian palazzo provided accommodation for students and priests, and was originally situated at Via del Cestari, in the middle of the city, five minutes walk from the Pantheon. Then it grew. More and more people learned about it, and the flat was full most of the time. So a new, purpose-made hotel-type establishment was proposed and built in the outskirts of Rome. It was run by nuns and supervised by priests, mainly financed by the Vatican. It was the same old story: help was always available for those who got out of Hungary.

Here we met Clarissa, who had early retired from Papua a short while earlier. In 1948, Clarissa had managed to escape from Hungary's budding communist regime to work in Australia, then in Papua and New Guinea, although her PhD in Philosophy did not seem a very useful qualification. She was also very beautiful, and had eventually landed a job to maintain her mother and herself. They had been planning to find something more permanent in Rome, but her mother had recently been knocked down and killed by a car. Clarissa stayed on.

Then we arrived. We had a lot in common, having lived the expat life at

Andrea's first communion, in Rome

opposite ends of the world in ex-British or Australian influenced colonies, while Lily and Andrea, who spoke only broken Hungarian and no Italian, were pleased to have someone to speak to in their mother tongue. We struck up a friendship which lasted until her death.

Eventually Clarissa settled in France, with frequent visits to England. She stayed with us several times, and kept on asking when we could spend some time with her on the Cote d'Azur. About ten years later we took up her offer.

Packing for the rest our journey became a bit more difficult. I couldn't tell any longer where exactly things were. But at last, the moment arrived when we crossed the Channel. The customs officer at Dover took one look at the dishevelled family with two youngsters, and the untidy car, and he waved us on with a rather conspiratorial smile. Well and truly, we had nothing to declare.

It seemed a long way from Dover to London, especially the last stretch. I was looking forward to being back home in Fulham, where our friend Anna, who had faithfully corresponded with us during our three years in Guyana, was expecting us. It was thanks to her that I didn't pack our bags and leave with the children during the difficult periods of our marriage, when the tropical heat didn't help to calm stormy matrimonial waters. She was a wonderful friend to me. As we pulled up, she came out from the garden, and there were tears as we hugged each other.

Our flat looked, and felt, tiny after the spacious houses abroad. It was small, very small for four people, and the girls were three years older and bigger. A few days later, our enormous travel chest arrived. While we were out, the carriers had dropped it in front of the house on the roadside, where it had split. When we got home, we found some of our things in the middle of the road. The cars must have been very careful not to drive over them, and nothing was missing. I was hardly able to unpack and find room for our belongings, as we were already bursting at the seams.

Something would have to be done.

Life, Day by Day

We knew we had to find a bigger place, and we soon did. It was 22, Gowan Avenue, across the road from Aunty's house. Three years earlier, just before we had left for Guyana, we could have bought a similar house around the corner for £6000. There was very little time before our departure, but it would have been possible to complete, and we could have let it, the same way we let the flat. However, Tam wouldn't hear of it. Now we were about to buy a house for £18000, in the same street where we had had our first London flat as students, and the same street where some years later Jill Dando was murdered.

The Building Society considered us big earners, and they were quite prepared to lend us the money we needed. By this time, a wife's earnings were taken into account for a mortgage - unlike a few years earlier when I couldn't even buy a bed on the hire purchase without Tam's signature. Anna bought us out of 49 Woodlawn Road, so we had no problem there, but the new large mortgage made me somewhat apprehensive.

We both liked the new house, but there were arguments. I would have liked the children's bedrooms on the first floor with us. In the loft there were two very small rooms, which could have easily been knocked into one to become Tam's study, - priority number one. But he wanted the bedroom on the first floor, overlooking the garden. I was afraid of losing the house, so I agreed, and the children had the rooms in the loft.

I designed a study for him yet again, complete with built-in shelves, storage units, drawers, you name it. Mr Kelly, our friendly Irish joiner who did a lot of work for us in Woodlawn Road carried out the work. By now, Tam had acquired a proper writing desk. It was placed in front of the window, so he could gain inspiration from the garden, which I looked after in my amateurish, beginner's way. I was no gardener but I loved it.

The Back of the House and Some of its Inhabitants

Only after his study was completed could I fit out our kitchen, helped by Mr Kelly. Needless to say, my drawing board was parked at the back of the through living room, by the French doors leading to the garden. I started to do some private work, but without a private space to myself.

Life was rather pleasant in the new house. We used to invite friends for dinner, and then probably bored them to death with our cine-film shows of South America and ourselves in the jungle. Usually, we had a session before dinner with drinks, and another after the meal. When we left for Guyana my father had given us a Russian made 8mm standard cine camera, and we had quite a few reels of films. When one side of the film was exposed, we had to turn it over, like the cassettes. If you forgot, one side was exposed twice over, and the film became quite psychedelic. I learned to edit and I spent hours and hours threading the projector. This was before automatic threading.

We settled into a new routine. There was no school run for me any more. Lily and Andrea walked to their schools, and they settled well into the new system. I was working part time, and if I was held up Aunty gave Andrea a drink and a home made cake by the time I got home.

Tam and I usually drove together to Bloomsbury. He worked in University College Library, and I got a job with a small architectural practice opposite the British Museum. It was a friendly crowd, including Ted, one of the partners and his eventual wife Anne, who used to be our permanent temporary secretary. Anne and I were the only women in the set up, and we became friends. The only thing I disliked was the smoky atmosphere. In a relatively small room there was nothing I could do but cough. I still think my asthma originated from those days. Work was good, though very developer orientated. Among other things, I had a job of putting up nine town houses in North London to replace four nice old spacious semis.

Then there came a call from the firm I had worked for before we went to Guyana. My favourite boss inquired if I was free. But I wanted to see my present job through, therefore I said I could only come a few months later. Mr Ratcliff could not wait that long. It was a mistake on my part, but the offer certainly made me feel eight feet tall.

Holders Hill, London. 9 new town houses

In the meantime, Tam was growing restless in his job at University College. In Guyana he was the chief and the undisputed boss in all library matters. He did not have to consider a team. Back in University College, London, it was of course different, and I believe he could not settle down. He started to apply for new jobs. I made it quite plain that I would not go abroad again unless he was seconded from his present job. The uncertainty of an appointment on contract without the security of knowing that at the end of it we could come home didn't appeal to me. In any case, the girls were just settled in their new schools. Tam didn't want to go away on his own, so we stayed. After a while, he was successful, and had an offer from the North London Polytechnic. Everything looked rosy, but clouds were gathering on our horizon.

My father visited us in the summer of 1973. He was our first visitor in the new house, and he liked it. We were very pleased to have him, because the year before he had had that heart problem, and then we had parted with very heavy hearts not knowing what the future would hold. By this time Tam was behaving strangely. Mood swings became prominent. He and my father spent hours discussing Tam's problems at work, real or imaginary.

For the past three years he had been free of depression. However, it seemed as if he was heading for a breakdown. The symptoms were familiar to me. He didn't want to go back to the psychiatrist who treated him a few years earlier, instead he wanted to devise a cure for himself. Off he went to do deep sea fishing. Then he took a group of librarians on a trip to Italy. None of it helped, of course, and he came home worse after each try. Neither did things go well at his new job. There were personal conflicts. Although he was Librarian, the establishment was run by the Heads of the various departments, and decisions regarding the library, like everything else, had to be reached by consensus. Tam was not flexible enough to negotiate. In Guyana, he was used to being very much his own boss.

Depression was still a taboo subject. Eventually, he returned to Banstead, the same hospital where he had been treated earlier. At home life had to go on. I was worried sick. We had a new house, with a large mortgage that I could not keep up on my own, should the worst happen. His specialist told me that he would be back in five weeks time, and able to work.

Visits to the hospital were difficult. When he came around sufficiently from electric shock treatments, he wanted to see the children. A psychiatric hospital is hardly the place for young girls. Thirteen year old Lily understood a lot, and she was very helpful as a young teenager. I believe Andrea was too young to understand the full situation, although she too must have been affected by the general level of stress. On his birthday, however, I took Lily and Andrea to see him, and I baked his favourite cake, a very rich recipe from his grandmother. Its base was of whipped cream which cemented together pieces of sponge and crystallised fruit. We all enjoyed the treat, and the hospital let us have some privacy. The girls didn't have to see the other patients.

The consultant was right: Tam was back at home in five weeks. He was prescribed a drug to replace missing lithium in his blood. Or so I understood it.

He went back to work, but the conflict was not resolved. Teamwork and dealing with committees required a lot of flexibility. Tam was suspended on full salary until he found a new position. It was quite a generous deal, but still I was worried. They were very understanding in my office, and Aunty was a tower of strength in those troubled days.

I could not discuss manic depression with anybody but Anna. Being a trained nurse, and a close friend, she lent me her shoulder to cry on. She was very knowledgeable about psychology and psychiatry, and she kept me going.

By next summer, Tam was well enough to have another holiday in Hungary. This time we drove. Tam left with Lily for Baja, and I stayed in Budapest at my parents' with Andrea.

Ivan's visit to his elderly mother somehow coincided with our visit. He contacted us and I accepted Ivan's invitation to join him for dinner.

"Would you like to hear some real gipsy music?" Ivan had asked. "I am sure Andrea has never heard any. Up on Castle Hill they play every night."

"O.K., let's go. And are we going Dutch, as we did with our coffees about 25 years ago?" I teased.

"That will certainly not be necessary. No way are you going to pay when you are with me," was his serious response.

We crossed the Danube on Adam Clarke's chainbridge, a replica of the Menai Bridge, then climbed up the hill. I wore high heeled sandals and I suffered as a result, while the other two happily skipped along. It was a very posh restaurant, and as 'foreigners' we received even more attentive service. The reverence for hard currency was embarrassing..

Wine flowed; the food was first class, the leader of the gipsy orchestra played requests at the tables. Andrea recognised tunes which she had heard before, and she was quite happy. We reminisced, and then talked about our present life. Ivan was single – divorced, he mentioned casually, and I confirmed I was a happily married mother of two - or at least, that was the impression I gave. The atmosphere was charged.

"But why isn't Tam with you?" Ivan asked.

"He left with Lily, our older daughter, for the part of the country where his family lives, while I am visiting my parents in Budapest," I explained.

"Aha!" The evening continued happily. Then we parted company, and went on our sweet, separate ways.

Within months Ivan remarried, and they had a daughter. He used a photo of his little girl as a Christmas card, as I had done for many Christmases. Our correspondence continued.

Why Manchester?

Tam stayed at home and started to apply for jobs. It was quite strange to have a house husband. He soon had several offers. I would have loved him to accept the one at Surrey. He would have had to commute, but at least we could have stayed in our new home. He didn't want it. He accepted an offer from Manchester University Library, and at the beginning of summer 1974 he started work there, staying in digs, and coming home at weekends. At first he flew, then he switched to the train, and finished up coming home by coach on Friday evenings. Economy had to be considered.

Lily started her O-level course at Lady Margaret's in Parson's Green. She was doing well. It didn't seem a very good idea to move her again. Andrea was only nine years old, and I didn't see much of a problem there. However, I wanted to wait and see how Tam's job would work out before making any further decision.

Summer approached, and we both had three weeks leave. That is a long time to be out of the office when you work part time in a small private practice. We were wondering what to do for holidays. Tam had not seen some of his family since before we went to Guyana. For some odd reason, we decided to travel by train to Hungary. Lily will never forget the Hungarian 'express' doing about 25 miles per hour in soaring temperatures when I had advised her to travel in a jersey trouser suit. I will never live it down.

We did the usual things, visiting both families and meeting old friends. Ivan turned up, all the way from the States. It didn't occur to me to ask what brought him to Budapest just then. Or perhaps I knew perfectly well, but I didn't want to admit it.

Back home, we were ticking over quite nicely until the 1974 recession hit the world of architecture. It was natural that the last one in, the part-timer, should be the first one out. I had a very generous deal, the firm offered to let me stay until I could find another position. This was decision time. It didn't make much sense to look for another job in London. We agreed that I would look for something in Manchester, and when there was an offer, I would move with the children to join Tam.

For the next few weeks I closely watched advertisements in the architectural papers. There was a position advertised somewhere in north Manchester: a small private firm invited me for an interview. I arranged for a friend to stay with the girls while I went away. Tam had lodgings in Fallowfield, south of the city centre, and I had no idea how to get from there to Heywood. By the time I found out, I honestly wished they wouldn't offer me anything. They did. I hedged, knowing full well I was not prepared to commute the distance.

There were three interviews booked for my next trip. Having worked with London County Council for years was a very good recommendation for any local authority job. Both Manchester City Council and Trafford Borough Council made offers. Manchester wanted an architect in their Planning Department. A job like that is not a big deal for an architect, but when I walked through the main gate of Waterhouse's Town Hall in Albert Square I knew I wanted to work there. I fell in love with the building. I thought it could only be good for an architect to work for an organisation that looked after its headquarters the way this building was looked after. And I wasn't far wrong.

But they say it never rains but it pours. I now had *two* offers from two local authorities, and one from a small firm in Didsbury. It was very tempting to work in Didsbury, considering my domestic arrangements. It was only a couple of miles down the road from our new house. However, I didn't want to be the last one in, first one out again, should there be further recession in the profession. I accepted the Local Authority position.

Leaving Card (kiosk for the Evening News designed by me)

The Next Move

Meet Manchester

My husband, Tam, got himself a new job,
and from now on Manchester will be my lot
though for long years I've lived in London
and in all that time, have not known boredom.

I apply for a post as an architect
at the Town Hall. I am selected,
and land a job to survey and plot
street by street, each and every green spot

as the Planning Department wants to know
where all the trees in the City grow.

Sunshine or rain, with a board in my hand,
I register trees, and mark where they stand.
When green grainy twigs leave me mystified,
I pick the leaves which I can't identify.

It is fun to explore this, my new town,
And I find superb buildings all around.
I soon fall in love with Manchester,
(though I wished for a tree in St Anne's Square!)

When I go into to the university's world
vistas and buildings become a bit blurred,
but I find that green areas have multiplied-
so pleasant for students and passers by.

What's more, Manchester pays me to walk up and down-
Praise be to the Council for all this fun!

Two Houses

I accepted Manchester City Council's offer, and I have never regretted it. I thought I had the best job in the world.

My first assignment was to carry out a survey of the city centre, showing the heights of buildings in relation to open spaces and trees. I was put in charge of the project, and I was paid for walking around and looking at this very interesting city while recording it. What better way to learn about a place? But I also had to identify trees. I had no problems with the buildings, but trees were another matter. I used to go back to the office holding branches and leaves, which I asked the landscape people to identify. In the end I had a schoolgirl's collection of specimens, stuck neatly in a copybook. In due course, a map emerged showing the results of the survey. Everybody was happy. An interesting picture emerged which showed very nicely where the city had its "breathing spaces". The University area won hands down.

There were weekly meetings with the architect's department to discuss all the pros and cons of the incoming planning applications. I felt a bit as if I had turned from poacher to gamekeeper. The meetings took place after lunch. My counterparts often had a few pints with their lunch, and the effects lasted to the end of our meetings. We were usually in high spirits. They treated with good humour one of my announcements - that I wasn't able to comment on a particular application.

"Why in heaven's name can't you?" asked the Chief Building Inspector.

"The application comes from the father of my daughter's boyfriend. I could be considered an interested party," I answered.

They roared with laughter, and we recommended the application for approval.

I was now back in full time work after a ten years gap as a part-timing Mum. However, on the home front I needed help. The thought of the girls coming home after school to a new and empty house was unacceptable.

Then I met our invaluable Mrs Green, whose family had just migrated to Canada. Her granddaughter, Angela, was the same age as my Andrea, and Mrs Green missed her granddaughter. Before the family emigrated she used to look after Angela while the parents worked. Now she found a substitute family, and she stayed with us until her health failed. She was in the house every day when Andrea walked home from school.

Andrea was happy in her new school, where the head was keen on swimming. She was a good swimmer. The school team was entered for, and won, every inter-school competition. Tam was very proud of his daughter. In his youth he used to swim, and played water polo for Hungary's junior team. Then, in his student days, he had continued at the University of Cardiff. I used to swim a bit as well, and I usually accompanied the team when they competed against other universities. So much so, that on one occasion in Swansea, the girls' captain came up to me and asked if I would help them out, and get changed since their relay team was not complete. As long as I could swim two lengths of breast stroke, they could race. I was four or five months pregnant at the time, but we made it.

Andrea followed in our footsteps, but a couple of years later she nearly broke her father's heart when after a race her team was interviewed, and she said no, she didn't want to become a swimmer. She didn't want to train seven days a week, sometimes twice a day, when there were so many other things to do in life. She was about ten years old.

Lily was doing well in her new school: she won prizes, and she was determined not to acquire a Mancunian accent. She played a bit of tennis, but she wasn't really settled. Like me, Lily had not wanted to leave London, and I wonder if the change affected her. She was preparing for her O-levels, and we didn't expect any problems. We were very pleased when she passed with flying colours.

The following summer Tam produced an ambitious plan. He wanted to canoe down the Danube from the Black Forest to the Black Sea. His sporty cousin would join him in the adventure. The plan was for me and the children to drive along, and camp near the river once they had put the boat in the water. When the time came, the men put the canoe on the top of the long-suffering VW Variant, and the two of them went off. We women went by train, to pick up the car in Germany. It was left with friends not far from the men's starting place. I didn't try to drive along their course, I dropped that part of the plan. I took the quickest way to Hungary, where my father had a weekend house on the Danube, about 20 miles north of Budapest.

Tam, who knew the place very well from previous visits, knew we would be there, and they had to pass by. But day followed day, and there was no sign of them. Then, one hot afternoon, two figures approached. One of them was a distant neighbour. He wanted to establish if we knew the other, who claimed he was looking for his father in law. He was a bit suspicious of this character, who was of very unsavoury appearance: unshaven for days, not exactly clean, in a rather worn out white pair of shorts. He had just got out from a canoe and enquired for my father. The neighbour wanted to be sure my father would be all right. Other people on the river bank had simply denied knowledge of my father, who was quite well known in the neighbourhood because he did a lot of work in the interest of the village.

A few days later, the men took to the water again, and paddled through Budapest, then to Baja, Tam's home town in the South quite near to the border with Yugoslavia.

However, the border guards didn't let them through, since Andrea, who was in Tam's passport, as she was in mine, was not with Tam in the boat. Lily had her own passport by this time. We could never understand the thinking behind this. Did they think Tam wanted to abandon Andrea in Hungary, or what?

To cut a long story and a holiday short, Tam left the boat in Baja and joined us. His companion flew back, and eventually we drove home.

In the autumn we bought a small three bed-roomed terrace house in Fallowfield. The City Council let me have a mortgage in my own right, although they knew we still had our joint mortgage on our house in London, which was let. It was a constant headache. Little did we know that holding on it would have made us millionaires! As it happened, when we finally sold it we put the money towards buying the house next door to us in Manchester. Our very elderly neighbours left, and we were all pleased not to go through the usual process of buying a house through an agent. We had now two double-fronted terrace houses, and I had a lovely time altering them. I broke through on both ground and first floors. We could walk across on the ground floor, go upstairs and come back on the first floor through a door in a built-in bedroom wardrobe. It was fun. We had six bedrooms, and there were times when I woke up in the morning not quite remembering how many guests we had staying under our roof.

Of course Tam requisitioned the new big bedroom for his study. For the last few years he had had to be content having his desk and his books in our bedroom. However, he rather resented the idea that I also wanted a study to myself.

"The whole house is your territory," he used to say. My large drawing board occupied a corner in the through living room where I did private work in my spare time.

Andrea on the canoe

Now that I had converted the two houses into one large one, Tam wanted to let part of it. In the past, when we could have done with a bit of extra income, he had always objected to letting. We did have a tenant for a while, but when he left, I simply moved my drawing board into one of the previously let rooms. And that was that. I loved it.

We had some trauma with Lily´s mock A-level exams. One day she mixed up the time table, and wasn't prepared for the scheduled exam, so she ran away to her boyfriend at York University. Eventually, of course, she came home and knuckled down to the rest of the work. She made no mistakes during the real exams, and by the following autumn she was at Birmingham University studying law. We were very apprehensive about her going away, as I didn't think she was ready for it. We also thought that Manchester had a much better law course. But living at home was as unfashionable then as it is now. As it happened, she didn't complete her course in Birmingham, but changed to London's Slavonic Institute, where she did a degree in Hungarian, gaining an upper second, and eventually a job with Radio Free Europe in Munich.

At work, after a time I was longing for a more productive position. The advisory schemes we did in the Planning Department were not the 'real thing' in my eyes. Being an architect, I wanted to build. I was lucky - after about two years the City Architect's Department had vacancies. There were nearly a hundred applicants, but I think it was due to those after- lunch meetings that I got one of the positions. Actually, Mr Shapley, the Assistant City Architect, came to me straight after my interview and told me that I had got the job. I stayed with the department for eleven years.

Gathering Clouds

In the summer of 1982, Tam and I went on holiday without the girls to stay with Clarissa, whom we had first met in Rome about ten years earlier when we were on our way home from Guyana. She now lived in the South of France, on the Cote d' Azur at Roquefort-les-Pins, in a breathtakingly beautiful flat in a mansion converted into most unusual units. It was equally close to the sea and to the mountains.

Tam said he could squeeze in a week, but not longer, because of a conference he should attend, but I could stay for another week with Clarissa, and continue with our customary chats late into the night. It was agreed, and we flew out together. Clarissa met us in floodlit Nice, and took us to her village.

Tam duly left after a week or ten days to attend his conference. Or so we were told. He was very difficult during the holiday. Clarissa was surprised how much he had changed, and I couldn't figure out what was wrong. I only knew that lately he had not been very happy in Manchester's University library. There was a new chief librarian, and Tam didn't get on too well with him in spite of playing tennis together. It was quite a relief when Tam left, and I could have long 'girly' talks with Clarissa.

Once back at home, life went on in its usual track. However, the atmosphere was a bit heavy, like the air before a storm breaks, although there were no visible clouds. Tempers began to run short. We still had our usual social life, went out together, and had people visiting in the evenings. But on one occasion I snapped:

"Oh, not again! You've just dropped your briefcase, scarf and hat on the floor, and put that awful rust coloured tweed jacket around the back of a dining room chair! How many times do I need to tell you to put that jacket away? Even after the girls spilled food over it, you still want to put it there."

"I'm not going to go upstairs, just to please you." And Tam went towards the kitchen to make his habitual cup of coffee before disappearing into his study to do his own thing.

I was already wound up. Having got home from work before him, I had started to tidy up. Lily and Andrea had finished their tasks, and they had even laid the table for dinner.

"Never mind pleasing me, just help for once! Although a bit of exercise wouldn't do you any harm, either. It isn't me putting on weight, you know."

"I have my jobs to do, you have yours. Lay off me!"

"No, I don't think so. It is your friends who will soon be here, and it is me who is left with all the work as usual. You just want to arrive like another guest. It's just not on. And have you got the drinks?" Although it wasn't a special occasion we should make the best of it, I thought. "Is the wine in the fridge or decanted? It should be red wine, with the dish, but just in case one of them wants white, that should be chilled. Do we have any beer? How about thinking ahead a bit? Not just doing your own thing."

"You're very good at giving orders, how about you taking some for a change?"

"Right, what would *Sir* have me do now?"

"You could have more time for me, for example."

Words flew fast and furious, and Lily and Andrea disappeared. It was getting quite unpleasant. Recently these quarrels had become more frequent, usually over nothing very important. But somehow we had less and less patience for each other. I was upset, and very angry. I was seething inside and tears welled up. I thought I would have to do something one of these days to make Tam realise a few home truths.

However, this time we had to stop. I wanted to have the house in reasonable order - but that didn't matter to Tam. Any minute now the bell would ring, and we didn't want people to know the seriousness of our arguments. Not yet, at any rate. So, I wiped my eyes, put on some lipstick, and Tam stormed upstairs with his cup of coffee. The stair treads thundered under his feet.

Just then the door bell rang. I was aware of the atmosphere in the house, whether the arrivals noticed or not. The occasion was not a formal dinner party, just dinner with the family, shared with two friends who were on their way home from work. I took their coats, and made an effort to be as pleasant as I could.

"Tam darling, come down, our guests are here."

"Yes, I'm coming," and the footsteps were considerably lighter than before.

"This is for the hostess," and Fred handed me a bunch of flowers.

"How kind of you, thank you very much."

"That's the least we can do for you. I hope you like it," said gallant Fred.

I managed to control my emotions, and after the general pleasantries remarked, "We could do with a drink - will you do the honours?" and Tam took the orders.

"Yes, I will have a scotch, it might calm me down, thanks."

"You are developing quite a taste for it, aren't you?"

"No wonder!"

Drinks helped the conversation. I was boiling inside, and wanted to do something about his non co-operation - that was how I saw Tam's attitude to our life together.

A little later, between drinks and serving a home made gulyás soup, I had a perfectly acceptable excuse for being absent, doing last minute tasks in the kitchen. It was then the idea struck me, and a little job took me outside the house.

It was still daylight when I went to the car, as if wanting something from the boot. The others sat in the lounge, from where they could hardly see me. I had opened the lid at the back, knowing no one would notice that it wasn't the boot but the engine of the VW. Looking after the car was one of my jobs too. Very early on, Tam had announced: "I am not technically minded, and you like playing with these things." According to him, whatever I did was because I liked doing it, not because it needed to be done. I took looking after the car seriously, and I went to a car maintenance class, where I had acquired some knowledge of the intricacies of an engine. Good as his word, Tam knew nothing about cars, and he wasn't a good driver. He had bought his driving licence in South America.

Now, I was going to put my knowledge into practice, and I went straight for a small piece, without which a car becomes immobilised. I had a sweet vision of Tam's face next morning. I was already gloating, and my anger began to subside. I was feeling much better. But then I didn't have the courage of my convictions, and after a time I replaced the rotor arm. After all, I would have to leave in the morning too, when timing might be difficult.

The gulyás soup went down well, followed by a pasta dish in a curd cheese and soured cream sauce with tiny pieces of pork crackling on top of it. Lily, Andrea and I liked to have it with sugar, not with crackling, so I served it both ways. Barbara liked it well enough to ask for the recipe. Or was she just as gallant as her husband?

Before coffee the children were excused and we settled in the lounge. To general approval I asked Tam, "Aren't we even having a liqueur ?"

A quick glance was exchanged between Barbara and Fred, and they said nearly in unison: "Yes, please, a brandy would be very nice."

So he served it.

"Just as well we are on the train tonight. Otherwise we would be well over the limit, after your treat."

"But look at the time, I didn't realise it was quite so late."

"We will miss our train, and the next one is much later. I don't think you would want us to spend half the night with you."

"I will drive you to the station," offered Tam.

" I can make up a bed for you," I offered.

"No, no thank you, we would rather leave a bit hurriedly if you don't mind. It has been a very pleasant evening."

" Thanks for coming, we enjoyed it too," and they were going to the car.

"Are you coming too?"

"You start to wash up in the meantime, you won't mind?" suggested Tam.

"Of course not," I hissed back and waved good bye to them, smiling.

He couldn't start the car.

" What is wrong?" I enquired innocently.

"It won't start," said Tam and got out of the car, standing helplessly by .

"Have you looked inside at all? What does it sound like?"

"It is dead. Do you think you could look at it?" Tam asked me.

"Just because you are not technically minded? Of course. Have you opened the bonnet yet?"

I opened it again and I fiddled for a while. No one took my activities seriously. Then I went back to the driving seat and started smoothly. Lowering the window I said:

"I can handle the car, you wash up."

The next day we were to attend a day-time parents' meeting to discuss Andrea's A-level expectations and university entries. Oh yes, Andrea was expected to do well, but oh no, Cambridge would be a very long shot for her.

We left quite happily, and Tam drove, dropping Andrea at home before we went back to work. On the way he quite casually mentioned that he had been offered a librarianship in Ireland at Maynooth. He asked me what I thought: should he accept it?

It was a bombshell. So this was why he left early while on holiday – not for a conference, but for an interview. He had never said anything about having applied for a new job. In the past we had talked about these things. We were in the habit of discussing everything, and not presenting the other with a *fait accompli*. I found this totally unacceptable, and very hurtful.

I thought hard. It became clear to me that he had gone this far without me on an important move, and what was more, he had even lied to me. Now, therefore, he must decide on his own, whatever the future might bring. I simply said that under the circumstances I was not going to be responsible for his decision. I reminded him he would exile himself for the rest of his working life. Nobody would offer him a job at a mainland university after a position at the Catholic University of Ireland, even though he was chief librarian there. And the Librarianship at a provincial university on the mainland was his ambition, though a few years earlier he had rejected an invitation from Colchester. It had come too soon after we had bought our second house in Manchester, and then he was happy in his job. Now, I was not going to ask him to stay, or tell him to go.

My instincts were right. When I had time to consider the implications for the family, I said that whatever he chose, I would certainly not leave Manchester until Andrea finished her A-levels and was settled somewhere. For myself, I wasn't very far for from early retirement age and a generous offer from the City.

His next question was would I go and see the place and the people in Maynooth. I had no problem with that. We flew over, and I promptly moved out of the hotel which had been booked for us. It was late November, cold and damp. The heating was almost non-existent, the bath tub bore the last guest's tidemarks, and there was a wedding reception with very loud entertainment clearly audible. I didn't even ask for another room. I wanted to leave. The next hotel was equally cold, but clean and quiet. An ominous start.

Then we went to the university, which had been upgraded from a Catholic theology seminary. It was a beautiful gothic building, with some original parts: pointed arches over stained glass windows, and wood panelling with ancient heavy furnishings. There was a roaring fire in the Jesuit high priest's room, and Irish whiskey flowed in abundance when he heard I liked whiskey.

He painted an idyllic picture. I listened, and asked a few questions: was this a permanent appointment?

Yes, Tam's appointment as the Librarian would be permanent.

What would his salary be in English currency?

The quoted figure was, in fact, worth less than his present salary, although he was only second in command in Manchester.

I made it quite clear that, as yet, I had made no commitment to follow him. If I were to come it would certainly not be before Andrea's A-level exams the following June.

I also wanted to know about work. I was not going to move to Ireland to peel potatoes like a good housewife. The Jesuit in charge found it a bit difficult to understand this. I think both of them believed that wives should follow their husbands, whatever. Naturally, they could not offer employment, let alone anything comparable with my Manchester position. But they would help. I was told there were plenty of opportunities in Dublin for an architect. And one very important question was left open - housing. We didn't really have time to look around. The establishment offered no help. One list from an estate agent indicated that houses were much more expensive over there.

Subsequently, I visited one of our suppliers just outside Dublin and had a heart to heart chat with him. As a result, my impression that this place was not for me was strengthened.

The only really positive outcome of a very inconclusive visit was a beautiful Irish green woollen suit I bought in Dublin.

Tam Leaves

On our return home Tam put the question to me again and again: "Do you want me to accept this offer in Ireland?" and I answered again and again: "It is your decision, I won't say."

With all this hanging over us we didn't have a very pleasant Christmas. Then Tam finally announced, against the advice of all our friends, that he would take up the job, starting after Easter.

We had a visitor booked for the Easter weekend, my old schoolmate, Ivan, who was over here from America. He had some work to do in London, and had asked if he could visit us at Easter, since he couldn't fly home to Nebraska just for the holiday. Tam was to leave for Ireland, so he would be in the throes of packing, but he foresaw no problem.

As the time of Tam's departure drew nearer, he decided for some reason or another to leave earlier than planned. He said he wanted to be settled in by the start of the new term. So he packed, and loaded the car the night before he was due to leave, because he needed an early start to reach the ferry at Holyhead.

Personally, I didn't think it was wise to leave a loaded car overnight in Fallowfield, where we could only park on the road. Of course, it was broken into, and half of the contents were stolen. My instincts were right again. All the same, Tam left. After the strain of the last few months it was a relief.

Ivan came, and we reminisced late into the night. Our friendship went back a long way. We were no more than teenagers when we first met, and had lots of shared experiences, good and bad. Our correspondence had continued for years, and therefore Ivan knew that Tam had accepted a job in Ireland, and that I was hesitant to follow. Before he left Manchester he told me that he was negotiating for

Tam, just before leaving

a position in London. It would be a step up in his career. He didn't get the post, but he was in London the following autumn.

As for Tam, nothing would ever convince him that he had mixed up the dates. According to him, I had manipulated Ivan's visit so that he arrived after Tam had gone. Not true. Time and emotions can play strange tricks.

Andrea was rather amused by these two oldies who had known each other since they were even younger than she was now. She was very busy preparing for her A-levels. At one point she said that she would not go to Cambridge even if they accepted her. She did not want to leave me quite on my own in Manchester, and Manchester University also had a decent French course. She was taking Hungarian, but only to make her application perhaps a bit more interesting to Cambridge. Although I was quite delighted to hear this, there was no way that I would accept her offer.

Lily was by then at university in London, and Andrea did get into Cambridge. Tam was not overjoyed to hear the news. I was over the moon. Eventually we packed my VW Polo with her things, including a new bike. We understood that everybody cycled in Cambridge.

In the autumn I got phone call from Ivan: would I care to meet him in

London? He wouldn't have time to come to Manchester. The same weekend, Arzén, another old friend from Guyana who now lived in Australia, was passing through London with his daughter, so I decided to meet them all in London. I only had to make arrangements for our dog, my only companion now that the house was empty. I was lonely, and very angry. The weekend away was more than welcome.

At Christmas, Tam and the girls came home, and we spent the holidays together as a family. But soon after we scattered again in our four different directions. My occasional visits to Ireland brought home to me that I did not want to live in Ireland, and that I did not wish to join Tam. He had made his decision without really consulting me. Of course, he had known that I would not move permanently to any other country. He said he wanted to test me. He did, and he got his result.

A few months later, I accepted Ivan's invitation to spend a week in Portugal.

With Andrea and her boyfriend in Cambridge

Later we met in Vienna and in Budapest, and so on. Of course, our illicit meetings were eventually discovered, and all hell broke loose.

To cut a long story short, and to save the gory details of our respctive divorces, suffice to say that we became singles again. Ivan and I met in our holidays for a couple of years, but eventually it was evident that the relationship was not going to work. The writing was on the wall, and we parted company. Ivan left America and returned to Hungary in the capacity of some kind of foreign expert. After a third American wife, he married a Hungarian lady. I never saw him again.

In the milleneum year I travelled with friends to Dubrovnik. On our way back by train from Zagreb to Budapest the mother of all storms followed us. Luckily it had stopped by the time we reached Budapest.

Next morning the phone rang. My brother, who lives in Budapest, asked if I had seen the papers or had listened to the news.

"No I didn't. I just about woke up after yesterday's long journey," I said sleepily.

"Ivan and three others were in an aircrash yesterday. They were travelling from Zagreb to Budapest in a private four-seater plane. There was a storm. There are no survivors. Watch out for further news, " he suggested.

I was silent for a very long time.

It has never been sorted out exactly what happened. Ivan's mobile phone was found intact on the ground with messages in it. It fell out of the stormy skies at a spot near to the railway line where I had been travelling at about the same time.

A Camper-Van Arrives

It was late November, following Tam's departure - one of those early winter evenings when the temperature dropped to unseasonable depths. The clocks were already put back to winter time keeping, and it was dark and cold as I was coming home from work. I knew the house would be empty, Andrea was in Cambridge, Lily was in London and Tam was in Ireland. The evenings were a bit bleak.

I could not park my car in front of the house - there was no drive to our terrace house, and a camper-van stood at the front. I saw a figure in the camper-van, but I took no notice of him. I was about to unlock my front door when a voice I seemed to know called out, "Hello, Gigi," and Arzén, our old friend from Guyana, climbed out of the van.

"What on earth are you doing here?" I asked, rather surprised since I knew that he and his family were living in Australia, though they spent long holidays in Europe travelling in this VW camper.

It seemed that at the end of this journey, the rest of the family had flown home, while Arzén crossed the Channel to park the vehicle at some place near Dover. But the place had closed down while they were away, and Arzén was stuck.

"It occurred to me," he said, "that the Kabdebos in Manchester would be the people to help out, so here I am, and I hope you're not going to throw me out for having come completely unannounced. I tried to ring you both, but you were out of your office, and the library informed me that Tam doesn't work there any more. There seem to be some changes around here."

Of course I didn't throw him out; actually I was quite pleased to have company. I duly made enquiries, and my octogenarian bridge partner offered his garage for the camper-van. He was not using it any more, so it was standing empty.

Arzén could leave his vehicle there until the following summer, when members of the family would collect it again. And so the arrangement was made. His children came and went, then family friends collected the vehicle, but Judy, Arzén's wife never appeared. I often asked what was happening, but the answer was usually evasive, except once, when Àgi, their daughter, poured out her heart, telling me how bad things were at home.

By the following summer, my own divorce, or at least separation arrangements, were taking shape. I moved to one of the two conjoined houses, and Tam came and went from the other one whenever he visited in Manchester. I had knocked the two houses into one, years earlier, not even dreaming of the consequences.

Arzen & the Camper

Now in the throes of divorce we were to partition off the large house again, one for each of us. Tam, however, seemed to have little regard for this arrangement. He considered himself free to come and go as he pleased, and took ornaments, and pictures off the walls, even the clothes brush in the shape of an elephant's head – because he collected elephants, it was his!

Then one day, without even the courtesy of a knock on the door, Tam barged through the communicating door between the two houses. He didn't speak. You could have cut the atmosphere with a knife.

Arzén had arrived the day before from overseas, but his presence did not deter Tam in the least. After all, Arzén had only come to pick up his camper-van to go on the Continent.

I was rattled, shaky, near to tears. The stress was beginning to take its toll. When Tam finally left the premises Arzén turned to me:

"You can't go on like this, day in day out. Come to Hungary with me and visit your family. I 'm leaving the day after tomorrow, and I could give you a lift."

"I've made no arrangements to take annual leave," I said, quite pleased with the idea. "I wonder if I can go at such a short notice."

"Try to speak to your boss tomorrow. He will understand, under the circumstances," Arzén encouraged me.

My boss obliged, and by the following morning I was packed, and we were off before the usual raids started. I phoned my brother in Budapest who was only too pleased to hear about my intended arrival.

I had known Arzén for many years: the families were friends, and our children played together in Guyana. I had no idea he regarded me in any other way. His question: "And how do you envisage sleeping arrangements?" came out of the blue. Travelling in the camper of course meant sleeping in it as well.

"In our respective and separate sleeping bags, of course," I replied, without hesitation. He nodded, and this was respected throughout the journey.

It was an easy journey compared with previous trips on the Continent with my family, when after driving during the day, we had to put up the tent, after which I had to produce food on the camp stove, and later clear up, while trying to keep everyone happy and pretending to enjoy the exercise. In spite of my dark mood, and my gloomy thoughts of my marriage on the rocks, travelling with Arzén was tranquil, with no arguments. We shared the chores, and there was usually time for a quick swim in those rather cold Austrian lakes. Quiet understanding was in the air.

When we arrived in Budapest, Arzén deposited me at my brother's house, rather late in the night. I had a very good rest there, and I was able to prepare my parents for the impending divorce. However, a minor problem was how to get home. Arzén was going to stay much longer than my annual leave allowed, so I needed a one-way flight or train ticket. Single flights were much more expensive than returns, so finally I bought a return flight ticket, thinking that Andrea, being A. Kabdebo like me, might be able to use the return part some time later. Date of birth does not feature on the tickets. The following Christmas she did indeed use up the ticket, for a flying visit to Hungary. From there she had only a short train journey to Strasbourg, where she was studying for a year. It all worked out very well; and as soon as I got home, I had the communicating door between the houses bricked up.

Years passed, and the pattern of Arzén's arrival to pick up the camper was repeated every summer, until one day it dawned on me that parking the camper in Europe had been an excuse. He had never taxed me with his problems, but another marriage of some 25 years standing was on the brink. Arzén and Judy, his wife had been taking their holidays separately for some time, ignoring the questions from friends and relatives whom they had visited together in the past.

Agnes & the Camper

Then I moved house, and no longer had room for the camper to park. On Arzen's behalf, I negotiated its sale, but Arzén himself still returned. And I had to admit I awaited and welcomed his arrival with pleasure. From then on we travelled in my car.

It was not long then, before he confessed; "It is you I love," and after a short pause my answer was: "I will wait for you."

While we waited, we tried to spend our holidays together, staying at each other's places. This way we had more than two months a year to be together, until Arzén took early retirement and joined me in Manchester.

Life was good. I still had a few years to work after my first early retirement from the Property Services Agency of the Civil Service. The early retirement offer was so good that I could not refuse it. However, I needed a job for the next five years to be comfortably off in the end. We were in a recession in the middle of 1991 and it was not easy to get another job. I was then working on RAF officers' housing, near Belfast International airport, and I carried the rank of Wing Commander. Site visits to Ireland were sometimes somewhat dangerous, but I loved it. My only condition was that I should be able to fly home at the end of the day. I was not going stay overnight.

RAF Officers' Housing, near Belfast Airport

My next job was with Wigan Borough Council, and meant a considerable drop in salary. It did not matter really. I just did not want to start to draw on my pension as yet. Commuting was bad. I had never had to do it, and I certainly did not like the job. But five years later, I reached the mature age of sixty when I could retire again. At that point Wigan offered me the post I should have had when I joined them, but no amount of money could have made me accept. I retired again, on very favourable terms, and after that we thought the world would be our oyster.

Celebrations started as we had come back from another skiing holiday with Anna and John. Anna, who had owned the downstairs flat of our house in London, had bought us out when we left. We remained friends. By now Anna was married, and I was officially single, though Arzén was with me and we were soon to be married. We returned together from Chamonix to their house in Fulham - very familiar territory, a home from home.

A memorable birthday-cum-retirement celebration followed. Invitations had been sent out long before our departure, and Andrea had offered to organise the rest, as my retirement present. It was going to be a sort of open day, with a buffet lunch prepared by a young man who had been my daughters' childhood playmate in Fulham. And what a lunch it was! He produced a sumptuous treat, with drinks throughout the day.

On my 60th Birthday, with Andrea and Lily

At the appointed hour, the guests arrived, some from far afield. I felt honoured by the effort they had made. We hugged and kissed and even shed a few tears on the doorstep. One couple could not quite remember the house, after all, it was about a quarter of a century ago since they had last visited Woodland Road. Trude managed to find the house on foot, but then I had to drive up and down the road to find her husband.

There were about thirty of us eating, drinking chatting and reminiscing. Then champagne was served. Somebody hushed the general hubbub of conversation. Ted, a previous boss, turned friend, wanted to say a few words. He was pleased to congratulate me on my retirement - he said - in the hope I would cause no more trouble to the profession and to clients!

When the laughter subsided, I was asked to answer. "Speech! Speech!" they demanded. By then I had quite a lot to drink, and it certainly did have some effect on me in spite of the considerable amount of food I consumed. Oh dear, I thought, this would be bad enough if I were sober, let alone in my present state! However, I managed to say thank you to everyone for coming, especially those who had travelled from far away to celebrate with me. I thanked them for my presents and for this party. Then the words came to me:

"My aim in life," I told them "was to retire three times. Early retirement for the first time came five years ago from the Civil Service. I did a lot of work for them in Ireland under not the easiest of circumstances. I could not ignore the offer. This time, I early retired from being employed in Wigan, but not from work. I will continue on my own, without bosses, committees and commuting to an office. From now on, I only want to commute from our bedroom across the landing to my study, until I finally give up. And then I hope you will be able to celebrate with me again."

Refilled glasses clinked, and somebody started to sing "Happy birthday." I was pleased to see, however, that no sixty candles were in sight, and nobody knew it was a triple celebration for me. Now that I had reached sixty, we could afford to marry. The friends who celebrated with us did not know that our wedding day was already arranged back in Manchester. For me it was a triple celebration, and filled with very happy memories.

And so it happened. We were married, and together we built a hide out in Hungary on the river Danube, where we planned to spend the summer months. We also started to travel a lot, as if we knew it wouldn't last long. Luckily we had time for a few journeys before Arzén became very ill.

Austrian Christmas – 1997

When I arrived in Austria as a refugee I spent Christmas of 1956 in Salzburg. During the Midnight service in the Cathedral I made a wish, and just as I had wished, forty odd years later, I was here again, with Arzén by my side. We had planned an Austrian Christmas at Badgastein, my favourite place in Austria, in the snowy Southern Alps. The town, lying in a valley, was in the 19th century the watering hole of Austro-Hungarian aristocracy. Mountains towered on both sides of the small river. I had fallen in love with it at first sight. It was a spa town where people came to cure all sorts of ailments. Filled with hot spring water, steam rose from the open-air swimming pool, while the gardens around were covered in snow. If you have you never tried swimming in a pool surrounded by snowy paths, and ice capped mountains, you have never lived. Nothing is more relaxing after a day's skiing. And then take a sauna, to work up your appetite, in case you haven't got one yet.

I had also invited my brother's family from Hungary. Travelling would be easy for them, since it is just a long drive from Budapest via Salzburg. Arzén and I flew from Manchester to Salzburg. At the airport my brother Lacko met us, with a lovely, warm, bear hug. He had driven from Hungary with my young nephew Dani, and a couple of hours later one of my daughters, Andrea, flew in to join us. While we waited for her, we paid a quick visit to Salzburg itself, to the city which never fails to delight me.

They say that you should never return to a place, because it will not live up to its earlier magic. Not Salzburg, not for me. I was pleased to show them around in the limited time we had. It was getting dark as we came out of the Cathedral. Memories came flooding back. Then the unmistakable smell of glüh-wine brought me down to earth. They sold it in the open air in the square, where a Christmas Market was in full swing and you could buy just about everything. The stalls were not just ordinary market stalls. They were wrapped in tinsel and glitter, and looked festive, even elegant. Most of them were lit up by some of the candles they were selling. This lent an eerie, fairytale quality to the fading light. The smell of candles added to the overall effect. It was pretty, just as pretty as the Easter Fair I had seen with Arzén earlier in the year. Then, spring flowers had provided all kinds of imaginable decoration, now pine tree based arrangements delighted the onlookers and shoppers. Apart from the usual touristy mementos, I was seriously looking at slippers. Even these looked Christmasy. A gentle touch from Lacko told me not to look. I could not understand why, as I really wanted a pair.

We drove back to the airport, where Andrea's flight came in on time. We piled into the car, God only knows how: five adults with luggage for skiing, and all the goodies my sister-in-law sent, as if we were expected to be starving. They would have certainly incurred a surcharge, had they come by air.

We navigated quite well in the dark, through motorways to smaller roads and finally up a steep mountain road which took us to the hotel where Arzén and I had already spent four holidays. The first occasion was one of those last minute ski bookings when one knew the destination airport but was only told about the actual resort on landing. We paid for a two star hotel, and were allocated to the Alpenblick, definitely a three star establishment. I really wanted to show its delights to all my family. The owner, Frau Hirsch, is also the manageress. She was obviously pleased to see us, now for the fifth time around, and five of us at that. Her name suggested some Hungarian origins, and this was confirmed in the course of our stay. There was also a new girl, Claudia very glamorous, Frau Hirsch's daughter who had done a course in London. Her English was excellent, and now she held dance and movement sessions for the residents. It did a world of good after skiing to the aching backs, muscles and old bones.

We arrived without a hitch. The welcome was warm. There were kisses on both cheeks, handshakes and an occasional hug. Thirteen year old Dani remarked: "They are all so very friendly in this place!"

I wanted to show off the place, but there was hardly any snow on the ground. Next morning we went to make arrangements for skiing. They said there was enough snow up in the mountains, but at the bottom of the big gondola lift the ground was quite bare. There was no skiing right down to the town.

But next morning, very early, Lacko was woken up by Dani, who drew the curtains and stood spellbound in the window. The scene was transformed. Everything was white, fairy-story stuff. There had been a heavy snowfall overnight, and Christmas had arrived, white as white could be. From the dining room windows we could see the mountains across the valley and the pistes where we were to ski.

That Christmas Eve, the hotel invited us for drinks before dinner. During the day the tall tree was put up in the dining room, and Andrea joined the team of decorators. It reached to the ceiling just like the ones of my childhood, and it was a beautiful tree, finished to perfection, as my mother would have done it. Each piece of tinsel was put on separately, evenly spaced. And the candles were real - none of the automatic flickers of electric bulbs. These were real flames. Candles in their clip-on holders stood perfectly upright, carefully positioned to avoid any branches above. Lit sparklers were hooked around the candle clips. The effect was

Arzen, Lacko and Agnes at Badgastein

stunning. There were loud oohs and aahs from the table of the Americans, quieter words of concern from our neighbours, a family from Sussex, who had come with three small daughters. They were afraid of fire. I had always had Christmas trees with candles on them, and we never set the house on fire. We simply took care, as did members of the hotel staff in the Alpenblick.

The staff almost stood to attention while a very old, regal lady sang a few traditional carols, accompanied by the piano. I recognised the figure as the lady with snow-white hair who had a swim in the pool under our window every morning at half past eight. "Grandma is soon going to be ninety," I was told by her granddaughter, the glamorous girl who had recently joined the management. She must have had a lovely, powerful voice in her youth. Even now, in the hushed silence, her voice rang out and we were asked to join in. The words of the carols were distributed in English and German. "Stille Nacht, Heilige Nacht" never sounded more intimate.

The custom was that at the evening meal the choice of next day's menu was circulated. We were asked to mark our choices. It gave rise to laughter every day when we asked Dani to translate it for us from German. Then we wondered what the next meal would really be. The last evening we did not have the usual ceremony. I thought it was a little strange, considering that the Christmas Eve meal on the Continent is the equivalent of Christmas dinner in Britain. All misgivings disappeared as we sat down to our festive table. The silver sparkled in the candlelight. Seven courses were listed. We had small portions of every traditional dish so that we could eat our way through them all. A small steak of fresh carp followed the delicious clear soup, nothing like the enormous portions which leave no room for dessert. The sweets, small, like petit-fours, each in its own case, were piled high on a large plate in the middle of each table. There were at least half a dozen different sorts, all baked on the premises.

Later on in the evening, I had the opportunity to congratulate the old lady and thank her for the wonderful Christmas Eve which so much reminded me of those in my childhood. Speaking English, she proudly explained to me that she was Viennese and did not come from these parts. She had married her Hungarian husband, who was a wine taster to the court in the good old days. By that she meant the days of Emperor Franz Joseph - if I understood it correctly – because the conversation had by then switched to German. We had had several glasses of wine by then. After the First World War they left Hungary, and settled in Bad

Christmas Eve in the Alpenblick: Andrea, Agnes, Arzen and Dani

Gastein to run the hotel. It became a true family-run establishment, obviously extended several times, in traditional mountain style, with mementos around and about of the family's interests over the decades. I would have liked to hear a lot more about her days, stories and experiences as it is not every day one can have the pleasure of talking to a great old lady. However, it was getting late for her.

I was secretly hoping someone would suggest we attend midnight mass. The church was half way down in the valley, a rather steep climb. But Andrea, who in normal circumstances would have been the most likely advocate for the midnight adventure, was still limping badly after a tumble on the slopes. Instead, we continued our private celebrations in our room. There was still a little space left for the traditional Hungarian walnut and poppy seed rolls Lacko had brought with him, washed down with first class wine also brought from Hungary. After that, we could have hardly managed church-going!

Then we opened our presents. Mine must have been the best: another fulfilled dream, and several pairs of slippers!

Round Trip to Bilbao

Arzén was diagnosed with Parkinson's disease, and life became a bit difficult, but we were coping cheerfully when the newsletter of the local chapter of my professional organisation dropped through the letterbox. I had retired in 1996, but I kept in touch with them. I nearly dismissed the letter as the usual sort of communication, not expecting anything very interesting. In the past I had attended some of the outings they had organised, which I had found were well chosen, well organised, and interesting. And indeed, this time there was something worth considering: a mini cruise to Bilbao on P&O ferries for the princely sum of £59. Two nights and a day in between on the boat, each way, and a day to spend in Bilbao. It might not be everybody's cup of tea, but it appealed to us. With luck, the Bay of Biscay would not be too rough. 'Please register interest by such and such a date.' I did, immediately. For a long time we heard nothing about it, but eventually our tour was confirmed.

My brain raced ahead. Why not make a grand tour of the occasion? Arzén hardly knew this country, and we had various invitations from friends in the South. Wasn't this the very opportunity to take these up? After a few phone calls, the route took shape. The Bilbao trip started in Portsmouth. It makes good sense to go from Manchester to Portsmouth via Plymouth, doesn't it!

We had a whole day to drive to Plymouth, if we chose to. Nothing like the nonsense of years ago when I had picked up a brand new car in Liverpool docks in the morning, brought it to Manchester to register it, and left for Plymouth at about 6pm. By the end of that journey I was so tired I could not find my friends' house, and had to accept directions from a total stranger. Over four decades of friendship my hosts were well used to witnessing odd behaviour on my part, but to arrive from Manchester about eleven p.m. with a strange man? Not an eyebrow was raised! They were about to welcome the young man in, when I explained that I had just picked him up in the city centre, where I was completely lost. He had said he knew the district I was looking for, and he navigated me there. However, he would now have to be taken back. What was another fifteen miles or so, with the day's four hundred miles behind me? But Bob wouldn't have that. He got his car out and drove my saviour to his home.

Now, 15 years later, I was not alone. I would share the drive with Arzén, and we had plenty of time on our hands. We decided to see something of the country on the way, instead of trying to break speed records. We drove comfortably to Worcester and had lunch in a rather nice pub. The fact that we could not help overhearing our neighbour's not exactly subdued conversation did not spoil the lunch. A rather patronising young lady executive was giving detailed instructions to her male companion where to dine in London. Although he asked for addresses, he appeared to be very much the man of the world who knew perfectly well where to go, and what to do about it.

We calculated that we had ample time to visit the Cathedral. Clever parking arrangements - to the greater glory of Worcester's Traffic Engineers - allowed us an hour's free parking by the Cathedral. From books, I knew to expect one of the finest buildings of its kind, but I was not prepared for what we saw. It was overwhelming in proportion and in majesty, not to mention first class restoration. We are so proud of what we can build nowadays, structurally, and engineering wise. But how about the circular Chapter House, with its simple central column support? The pure simplicity and elegance of the space is barely matched by our all too scientific - I nearly said 'know all' approach to designed spaces. Arzén could hardly drag me away, but the parking meter was ticking. A quick look at the fine Romanesque crypt, which has survived from the time of the rebuilding of the original Saxon church during the 1080s, and we had to be on our way. We had planned to arrive before nightfall.

I thought we were sort of half way to Plymouth. I was wrong. We had a long way to go, not to mention the changing weather of a February afternoon and the increased traffic. We all know the feeling of being stuck in a traffic jam, unable to get to a phone. It was better to just get on with it and drive on. We did. In nasty driving rain, fog - everything! The stretch from Exeter was the worst, with window wipers on their fast setting, our eyes glued to the road, visibility very low and my back beginning to ache.

Plymouth at last! How good it was to arrive at the familiar house. This time I did not miss the way, and I was soon flat out on the sofa with a generous whisky in my hand.

The next few days flew past very quickly. Bob appeared every morning with a cup of tea and a cheerful "Good morning," - just like forty years ago! Although it was February, we were lucky with the weather. We took walks on Dartmoor, and on the cliffs around the coastline, which helped to blow the cobwebs away. We discovered a lovely pub that Bob and Beryl had eyed for some time, but had not yet managed to get inside. A real fire flickered in the old fireplace, and the beams of the low ceiling were real. So was the food!

Since all good things must come to an end, so did our stay.

Other members of the Bilbao party, unfortunate workers, left the North on the afternoon of the evening's sailing. We would leave that morning from Plymouth. It might be an equally long drive, but what a difference to have the whole day to do it. Besides, the Plymouth-Portsmouth run is much pleasanter than the M6.

The morning of our departure dawned, and after some reorganising of our luggage, we were ready for the road. We were not, after all, very likely to need walking shoes on board the *Pride of Bilbao*. We had consulted Bob and our maps the previous night, and reached Portsmouth without any trouble. Once there, it was a bit more difficult to find the right docks, the long term car park, and the place where we were to meet. At the appointed time, we noticed a vaguely familiar figure looking about, just as I was. We soon established that we were looking for each other, and for the others who had not yet turned up. So we joined Arzén in the main reception area where everybody would have to report before the group could board. They came at last, and finally we were all on board, duly introduced to each other. Then we noticed Arzén's overnight bag was not with us! I asked a steward if I could walk back to fetch it, because it appeared quicker to reach the terminal building on foot, rather than go by the bus route we had taken. Walk, indeed - it was more like 100 metres hurdles through the paths for staff only! The reception hall was fairly empty by now. I raced to the row of seats where Arzén had sat amidst our baggage. Luckily, his familiar grey bag was still there. Another quick march back to the boat, and then several flights of uneven steps up to the entrance - I was ready for a shower, whether or not I changed for dinner.

The following day passed on calm seas in glorious sunshine. The February sunshine was warm enough for us to sit on deck, wrapped in blankets. Members of the group met on and off, and we began to know each other. We passed around cuttings from various architectural journals about the building we were to visit

The package included several organised shore trips. Architects being architects, we wanted to do our own thing. It was the new Guggenheim museum in Bilbao we set our hearts on. For a very long time my favourite modern building has been the Guggenheim museum in New York, designed by Frank Lloyd Wright. I saw it when it was quite new, nearly thirty years ago, and I was overwhelmed by it. A circular ramp goes up and up, cantilevered from the perimeter wall of the building. The ramp provides exhibition space and the central volume with the sparkling gallery provides drama. All is nearly monochrome, off-white and as elegant as it could be. Would this new wizardry live up to its predecessor? The third or rather, the first Guggenheim museum is in Venice, of course. That is out of the competition, and I have yet to see it.

We docked quite early in the morning, well before museum opening times. A bus had been hired, it arrived on time to pick us up, and we were soon approaching Bilbao. We travelled through industrialised areas, which bore the signs of defunct heavy industry, due to perilous regional politics. Then we reached the city on the banks of the river. We passed large blocks of flats, packed in, close to each other in a sort of eclectic style. Balconies nearly touched, fresh washing hung on them and from the windows. A broad avenue led to the civic square with a large statue in the middle, where several radial roads met. Past the open space, we crossed the river to reach the museum car park, very much a building site. And there it was, in an implausible location on the riverside, a building that languidly scrolled and coiled before us.

A somewhat odd tower punctuates the museum complex. The area is to be redeveloped, to tidy up remains of industry. The old bridge, Puente de Salve, cuts into the new building - or rather, the new building tries to grow across the old bridge. We had plenty of time before opening, so we walked around. Away from the river, on the city side of the museum an enormous topiary dog was meant to break up the rather hard landscaping - an interesting form of gardening, and a good conversation piece. But it doesn't count as planting.

We walked across a new footbridge designed by Calatrava. It hangs from one single arch that sweeps diagonally from one side of the footpath to the other. It is a beautiful shape. When you look back from the river, the museum tower makes visual sense, looks good, and finishes the complex. And what a complex it is! They

An enormous topiary dog.....

prepared the drawings with aerospace computer technology. Various shapes and forms are thrown together, in creamy ashlared limestone, shiny, glittering titanium sheeting and glass. Nothing meets at a right angle, every corner is acute and mullions are not vertical. It must have been hell to supervise construction, and how it will all weather is the 65 million dollar question.

We could hardly wait to get inside. How does this building work, was the question on our lips. By now a queue formed at the entrance, which is below ground level. It is not placed in an easily recognisable position. We got through the cashiers, some of us with reduced price tickets, even without our birth certificates! Inside, the building opens up and comes to its own. A 50m high atrium, one and a half times taller than the one in New York, gives access to devilishly whirling volumes. Again, nothing is straight. Each room is of a different shape, and they are linked by twisting and turning ramps. It works. We all liked the inside, especially the way it gave intermittent views to the river.

There was a small hitch with our return transportation; our time was one hour earlier than the local time. Our bus driver was an hour late - according to us. What is an hour between friends, in the sunshine, in good company? Some were anxious and made their own way back to the boat, but we all arrived there in time for sailing. The following day of our return voyage was uneventful and not as nice as it was to head towards the South. Our thoughts were on our respective return drives.

Once ashore, we did not have to go far, as a London stop-over had been arranged, with our friends in the house we bought together, back in 1963. On Sunday, we decided to go to Wisley. This was a bit unfortunate, because it is 'never on Sunday' for the great public – Wisley is only open to members of the Royal Horticultural Society. So that was how we became members for six months, in order to be able to get in, and to take our two guests Anna and John with us.

Next day Arzén suggested we visit the rebuilt Shakespeare theatre. We had missed it during an earlier architectural trip to the site. By now we were able to see it in its full glory in a not very glorious part of London. It is a most authentic reconstruction of all English oak, not a nail in sight, just wooden pegs, as it used to be. Schoolchildren had a go on stage, performing snippets from Shakespeare plays. Our guide was an actor himself, with a most beautiful velvety voice.

The last stop of the round trip was Cambridge. I thought I knew London well enough to cut across to reach the M1. It took us two and a half hours! I will stick to the horrible M25 next time.

My friend Lisa had been trying to get me to visit her Cambridge home for a long time. We had worked together in Mycenea in Greece on a dig. She ran it for three summers with military precision. Arzén and I had spent holidays working there. Her house in Cambridge is 1930s architect-designed, built for her parents, a pure delight of domestic spaces, with immaculate detailing. We were told that the builder did not have to cut a single brick during construction. It had been listed not long before our arrival. I don't envy her the cost of maintenance, but I do envy the proportion of the rooms in her home.

After that, we turned our noses towards our own home, sweet home, where everything was in order. Nothing was burnt down, blown away, or broken in during our absence. The round trip to Bilbao was over.

Animal Sacrifice

Kathmandu

We were not to know that the Bilbao trip was our last together. Arzén's condition was deteriorating. We planned to go to India, where Arzen had spent quite some time in his youth. His father had worked there on an assignment, as an engineer. Now he was not interested. In the end, he decided to go to Australia to see his family, while I went with another three friends, Anna, John and Carmel, to India.

I sat next to a very tall young man in the middle seat of the jumbo jet. How he managed to stay folded up during the eight hours flight from Heathrow to Delhi, is beyond me. For me, it was uncomfortable enough to decide that I would not fly long haul again until couchettes are introduced on aeroplanes. We chatted, of course. He was going to Calcutta, adding a further few hours to his discomfort. He had been to the parts where I was going, and at the mention of Kathmandu his eyes lit up.

"You must go to Dakhinkali - it is a bit off the beaten track, but well worth it," he suddenly announced. He even wrote down the name of the place, although he was not quite sure of the spelling. It was named for Kali, one of the Hindu gods. "Is there anything special?" I wanted to know.

"Animal sacrifices. If you are not squeamish," came the reply.

So after all the official tours were over - and they did not include Dakhinkali - I went alone with the friendly Nepali Buddhist driver we had more or less engaged for our remaining days. He suggested that we go on Tuesday, because there would be fewer people than on Saturday, the other day for sacrifices. He was absolutely right, and he was more knowledgeable than the man in the hotel's tourist information office.

This taxi driver had never been to school. In Nepal, you don't have to read or write to obtain a driving licence. Driving is quite a different skill to what it is in Europe. Nowhere, not even in South America, did I experience such chaos. They pass each other within millimetres at the edge of precipices, calmly and quite safely. There is a six-monthly check up on cars, a sort of MOT in the form of a small bribe, which provides the police with a little extra to supplement their salaries. My rather knowledgeable driver earned £80 per month.

The horn is the mighty communicator. Without it, one can not overtake, warn, or greet one's friends. The general noise level in Kathmandu is quite phenomenal; only the pollution is worse. Some people wear masks on the streets. Our driver often said, "Madam, mask," and I would then wrap my white silk 'friendship' scarf around my head, to cover nose and mouth. The scarves were given to each of us on arrival at the hotel, a rather lovely, SAGA organised gesture. I even lined it with the refresher pads handed to us in the various aircrafts. It may have worked to some extent, but we all developed a Kathmandu cough. At least we did not spit!

We set out at nine o'clock. It was a hazy day, when the surrounding snow-capped mountains were not visible. We headed south, out of the Kathmandu valley. We passed the University, which I would have loved to see, because a few days earlier, on another trip, we saw a house with a sign: 'University Professors' House'. This was some twenty miles out of town, in the diagonally opposite direction, at Dhulikhel, a beautiful village just outside the Kathmandu Valley, providing a better view of the Himalayas than anywhere else in the valley. It would take nearly two hours to commute from there. Perhaps university professors have helicopters in Kathmandu, or the house is only for holidays. I did not get an answer to this question.

After about an hour's drive we came to the end of the valley, and to the end of the road. There was a quite spacious parking place, where my driver promised to wait for me. He instructed me to zip up my bum bag, and pull my sweater over it. Although it was Tuesday, and not the crowded Saturday, I should be careful, especially since I was alone, and not with a group. Thank Heaven for both, I thought.

A short walk downhill through the tall surrounding mountains led me to a clearing at the bottom of the valley. The route was lined with the usual hawkers, sellers of all kind of bric-a-brac to attract the tourists who, however, were quite absent, save for one quite well behaved group of about half a dozen Germans.

Colourful booths along the path

There were many more food stalls for the pilgrims, fresh vegetables beautifully arranged and freshly cooked refreshments. They fried all sort of delicacies over camp stoves or on cheerfully smoking open fires. It all smelt delicious.

One of the paths was signposted 'To the Kali temple'.

A winding path sloped up to reach the summit. I decided to go - after all this was what I had come for. The steps, 276 of them, were of brick, with some kind of cement poured over them. Scratched lines on the surface formed in a square sort of pattern, probably to make the steep steps less slippery. They would not pass Building Regulations, or any Health and Safety requirements, but they have lasted at least for the last nine hundred years. It was a sweaty climb: every bend promised the end, but that was rather elusive. No Europeans climbed up here, this was native ground. No one wanted to sell anything, no one crowded in on me. None of the usual high pitched voices chanted, "Hello," "Madam," "Very cheap," "Good price," in the way that was so unpleasant everywhere else. Only food was prepared up here, and served along the path, for the pilgrims who tucked it in great quantities.

A winding path sloped up....

Finally the Kali temple came in sight. It was a white circular structure, without outside walls, just columns supporting a flat roof, pierced by a large 'people's tree.' Its crown provided the cupola above, as nature intended. I was allowed to walk round the outside terrace, while Hindus prayed within, without shoes. Leather, shoes, photography and so on are not allowed at the altar. And you must be born a Hindu, you can not convert to Hinduism.

But where were the offerings, the animal sacrifices? And the service that goes with it? I had to descend the 276 steps to find the place.

Then other steep steps led down to a small clearing where Hindus took their shoes off and queued in a most orderly and quiet fashion, carrying their offerings. A little boy held a large brown cock in his arms. I wondered if it was his pet. I guessed he knew what was to come. A young man had two chickens tied together, swinging them, heads down. One of the worshippers had three sacrificial birds tied together. A duck peacefully hid its head in the soft feathers of a bigger bird, that seemed to be alert, and watched the proceedings. The third one, a large

The Kali Temple

cockerel, was restless and bobbed up and down. The owner kept on pushing his head down, trying to keep him quiet. There was apprehension in the air.

"Tourist, right!" A young guard pointed to me with no uncertain gestures when I wandered in the wrong direction. The place of offering is for Hindus alone, so I skirted around at a slightly higher level, on what one could call an observation terrace.

Sloping roofs covered the long benches on two sides of the square, where the offerings were placed. Garlands, fruits, rice and spices were placed in small compartments on special plates to be handed over as offerings. The quiet orderliness of the ceremony was remarkable.

A young man in front of the bench accepted livestock. With expert, swift movements he held the bird for a second in both hands with its head free to look around for the last time, before he bent back the neck. A quick cut with the large and, I expect, very sharp knife severed the head, the same way as I had seen it done in the countryside of Hungary. My sister-in-law had performed the same ritual not so long ago. That bird had been served for dinner in the evening. Here, a few drops of blood were sprinkled above the bench, as the offering to the God, and the still wriggling, now beheaded, bird was returned to the owner. Some of them asked for the head to be returned too. The offering finished up in a plastic bag, and the family retired to their picnic, surrounded by the mountains. Slightly dazed, I climbed back to the car park, to my patient driver, who whisked me back to my very different world.

On reaching home in Manchester, I was told that Arzén had had a break-down and was to be flown home, accompanied by a nurse. On the day of his arrival we had our GP, a rapid response nurse, and finally, a hospital consultant visiting us. The consultant suggested that we take Arzén into his ward at the Infirmary to establish how much of Arzén's confusion was due to jet lag, and how much to the advancing Parkinson's disease and dementia. Arzén never came home again.

After Arzen

Without Arzen

In Laurel Court

The hospital has discharged you:
they can do no more
to halt or slow down the progression
of dementia, linked to Parkinsons's desease.

So I found the home considered best for you:
lots of room for you to wander round
not stopped by corridors or walls;
a large room on your own;
a four-star hotel, even
a shopping mall.

Some of your belongings decorate the walls:
pictures of us, the family, and me, our next of kin,
mementos from happier years.
You don't seem to notice –
 Once only did you show a visitor around.

They say you are now settling,
communicating more in your shrinking world.
Some of your utterings are surprising -spot on-
And you answer the quiz questions
we could not solve the day before.

Then you get up without a word,
wander away in your own world
which I cannot enter,
no matter how much I try.

Your answers become a riddle
as if you are filling in a cross-word puzzle
the clues of which are in the past.
On some of them I can cast a light -
no one else understands.

When I see you, there is little to do.
You enjoy the fruit I take,
(to ease your constipation);
I sort your clothes, your shoes mixed up
with other shoes, and laundry tags and missing slippers.
And I still feel so useless.

You can negotiate the stairs, one hand on the bar
the other supported by my arm,
so in fair weather, we walk round the grounds,
doing our rounds. We even go to nearby shops
to keep you on the spot.

My mood changes every day
since you moved to this place,
depending on how I find you
when visiting every day.

Shopping

The days are strange.
No one there to wait:
no one who waits for you,
no one for you to wait upon.

No one opens the door
when I now come home.
My shopping bags are full,
but where are you?

The car door and boot lid are open-
Where is your helping hand?

You loved to rummage
through all those items
looking for the extra
special of the day
before I stored them.

In the happier days
we shopped together,
so that time spent on the chore
was not a waste.
We enjoyed each other's company.

'He is in Laurel Court,'
I tell the friendly shop assistants
when they ask about you.
' How do you cope?'
some want to know.

'Just about.' My staple answer.
Then I go home to cry
and write these lines
reaching for the whisky glass.

Resentment

I begin to resent
my dearest oldest friends
alive and kicking in their nineties,
and not shy of travelling to the Indies,

my pals on the courts,
aged over three score and ten
play better tennis
than I ever did.

The eldest, eighty-four,
got up after a fall.
A short stay in hospital
and again he hits the ball.

He's hard of hearing,
so we have to shout the score,
but the strokes are still there
and we all have fun.

Only you are missing-
barely older than me.
Your racket longs for tennis.
Your ski pants hang sad.

Bent back, and hanging head,
feeling along the hand-rails with uncertain steps -
my husband of less than a decade,
a human wreck. Can it be worse yet?

I try to tell you where I've been,
remind you of the club, the people.
Do we know if it sinks in?
Would it better to leave you in peace?

Question, test, caress and stimulate -
according to professionals, these will only agitate.
Feeling so useless, how can I
accept their advice, and not even try?

If It Was Death

When someone dies
there are no more eyes and ears
or word of mouth
to remember the past.

No more memories to trigger -
'Dearie, do you remember …?'
I search for clues and signs
from the twisted grooves of your mind

watching every word you utter -
does it make sense, or do you only mutter?
There is only one sign -
that beautiful smile.

that comes through and laughs
like a sudden floodlight in the dark,
a beam over foggy, black seas
from a light-house tower.

But when someone dies
there is no more laughter.

Death will be final on this side.
Will it release you from your plight
and bring relief into my life?

Death might not be the end as we think it
according to some beliefs,
for the hereafter will begin.
Oh God, help us.

Easter, 1999

I believe he is quite relieved
not to see, not to hear
in the dreary dank and dark
depths of his misery.

Lewy bodies on the brain
simply spread and invade
sparing nothing in their way.
There is nothing more to gain.

Feet totter, speech is a mutter.
Sometimes a smile lights up the eyes;
so painful, that old spark-
Do you know how I cry?

The years were fun with you.
I would even bring back this last stretch
if I could only have you not so bad
as it is now, with worse to come.

I have been through this before -
another man's depressions, decades ago.
Every time it hit, I was assured
that they could bring him back.
They did.

We were young, the children small
the confidence of youth was with us.
It was difficult, but not hopeless
Fear was the order of the day,
not hopelessness.

That was in another life.
Pollyanna says
there is always reason to be glad,
I can not see that yet.

Days pass fast. I have a task -
to change past happiness,
accept the present, face the future.
Give me strength.

Funeral

Life very rarely turns out as we would wish, and sometimes contrives to be downright unkind. Arzén died on 17th July 2001 only two and a half years after his return from his last voyage. His father had also died aged 69. Arzén lived one month and two days longer than he did, and just waited for his sister to arrive to see him. The day of his funeral coincided with Lily's birthday. This may have prompted Lily to write the following obituary:

Arzén was not a religious man, nor was he a person stuck on any particular traditions – although being married was clearly important to him.

Arzén was not a religious man, yet he held a deep belief in reason for the sake of it, warmed with an endearingly mischievous sense of humour.

Arzén was not a religious man, yet a man of deep, steady feelings with all the decorum practised by enthusiasts of the church. He required no external rituals as a framework in which to display politeness, respect and humility at all times. In him these qualities were natural.

He gave my mother a short dream – a mixed potion of important ingredients she had found lacking in her previous marriage. She had wondered if such a supportive mate was ever to be her fate and found it was – if only for a short while.

Arzén was not a religious man yet, he wore a permanent cloak of serenity. It had, perhaps, been folded around him by the spirituality of India where he lived as a child. To me, Arzén was always in tune with good spirits of some kind. He moved with them silently in life when well and more vociferously as a fantasy life took him over later on.

Arzén was a man endowed with tender, fatherly qualities – of which I was afforded an unforgettable taste over the last decade. Like mother, I too had been looking forward to the development of our acquaintance and was hungry for his gentle guidance and balanced view of life.

Maroon Balloons

Easter of 2001 brought welcome relief to my sad daily routine. Andrea was to be married. We went across to France where she had some connection with a shop that made wedding dresses much more cheaply than anywhere in Kent, or in Manchester, for that matter. We took the car across on the ferry, as Andrea lives only a few miles from the coast. I realised the night before our departure that I did not have my passport with me. There would be no problem getting out of the country, but how would I get back? We set out regardless, and we found her shop in a small town, and the dress was chosen - a very low cut, close fitting ivory dress with a burgundy jacket. All the accessories were to be burgundy or maroon. On the way back we tried to explain to a British immigration officer that I was neither an illegal immigrant, nor a stowaway, just an over-excited mother on a shopping trip for her daughter's wedding dress. A few bits of my available documents must have done the trick, and we were free to go. My respect for British officialdom has grown even higher.

Back in Manchester, I started to look for Andrea's special maroon balloons. I spotted one in a flower shop and later, after the wedding, it talked to me:

"Life was very pleasant in the scented atmosphere of this flower shop," it said. *I floated above the tallest stems, slowly swaying in the fresh air whenever the door was opened. Every time some of the lovely coloured flowers were taken away and replaced by fresh ones, I floated into a new position.*

Then one day you entered my life, looking exhausted as you came in. It was not flowers you asked for. Oh no, you wanted to know if I was for sale. My complexion was just what you had been seeking for some time, and you said I was beautiful. I was suddenly made to understand that I had many siblings in existence somewhere, in some other place, because you wanted twenty five like me and not those common silvery cousins of mine. My siblings were not round, shiny, filled out like me, but flat, flat, flat. Can you imagine it? On top of each other, crammed together in dozens in a plastic bag. There was some talk about my inside - whether it was of air, or helium gas. Helium indeed! It would escape in no time at all, through my fine, gently coloured shiny skin, Helium is for those big, silvery, rather common cousins of mine.

And how could we be transported? Transported, where and why? There was an agreement in the end to purchase all of us, uninflated - and you would also buy a pump, the life giving pump which keeps me nourished from time to time so I can keep my head up and smile. Although the shop offered to pump us all up, this was not a good idea, because we were to travel in a car, and we would have blocked the driver's view. And anyway, there were to be other people to share the space. In other words, there was no room for us in our full glory.

So, a few weeks later, my flat siblings arrived at the shop, and an ivory coloured cousin was inflated to general 'ohhs' and 'ahhs'. We were beautiful. You arrived, and seemed to be very pleased. We were given matching ribbons around our necks, to general admiration. But then, disgrace of disgraces! Even the two of us were starved of air, deflated and unceremoniously packed up. We were unconscious for a long time.

Then came the day when amongst much noise, surrounded by not nearly as many flowers as in my old home, you freed us. Oh, the fresh air! Not only from the pump, but even from people trying to act as pumps. Nowhere near as efficient, may I add! We soon filled up the house, and I just wondered what would happen next. It appeared that we were to go to a big place where there was room for all of us to float about. This time we were gently squeezed together in a dark compartment, not bad at all. We were tied together, ivory with maroon. The less fortunate ones were squeezed into black plastic bags and dumped into vehicles.

Finally we arrived at a very breezy place. I was worried about my inside and outside as we were sprayed just as they used to do the flowers in the shop. But there was no shop, no flowers. It was just cold and wet. Then I realised we were in the open air, and soon we went into the big place. When we got there inside it, it was like the old shop, but much, much bigger, and with fewer flowers. As they gently freed us, we caught our breath and the colour came back to our faces. We were arranged once more among flowers, rails and columns. Then it was all quiet.

But not for long. Many people came, and you as well. You looked elegant, and rather happy. The doors kept opening and shutting, and we could all sway in the air rushing in, to many oohs and aahs, like those we had heard before. Now I saw why we had to be in pairs of ivory and maroon. The girl right beneath us was dressed in a long, slightly shiny ivory dress and a maroon jacket which they called burgundy. There was also a little girl dressed the same way. She carried a bouquet, of - you guessed- ivory and burgundy flowers. We were not a bad match.

Later, when the room was empty, two ladies came and dismantled us. All the balloons were marooned except me, because I was given to you.

That night I dreamt that the other balloons were carried along narrow passages and stairways, through a bedroom and into a bathroom. Horror of horrors! Some of them landed in a basin called a loo, and most of them in an enclosure where they could hardly move between glass walls and the door. Drops of water dribbled from above. They were cramped and wet, until the girl in our colours came in with her new husband.

As they tried to come into the bathroom, seeing the balloons, they burst into laughter, until they fell into each other's arms.

Epilogue

Life Goes On

But as they say, life goes on. Arzén has been dead for nine years now, and in spite of many difficulties, I have rebuilt my life.

After the funeral I had a lot to think about. I was alone again, and I needed activities to fill the time I had spent visiting Arzén every day in the nursing home. I began by organising my days to be full. I had my own small private practice, and I took on any work that came along. What followed were very fruitful years, and for one client I even designed the house that I would love to live in myself. When I reached seventy, I achieved the aim in life I had laid out on my sixtieth birthday: to retire for the third time, and I started to wind down the small practice I had run for ten full, and very active years, with no bosses or committees, and only my clients to please. I had loved it, and quite a few of my clients remain my friends.

In this new kind of life I had time to take old ambitions of mine seriously. Mrs Roberts, my old patron, had died years earlier. Among other things she was a poetess, whose works were published in Austria. She had left a copy of her autobiography – a bound manuscript, *"Through Alien Eyes"*, to my ex-husband. Her wish was that Tam should arrange for it to be published. Nothing happened in twenty years, so it fell to me to try to do the job. I joined a writing group where Elizabeth took me under her wing to correct my 'accent' in writing (in other words to render my idioms into English). With her help in editing, I published 200 copies and it sold out. I have done my duty.

Another ambition was to put into writing my father's tape-recorded adventures in the Second World War. He spoke Hungarian, and I had to produce the English version of it. It took years, and much patient listening by the ladies of *The Thursday*

Group, before Elizabeth again edited the lot. We produced 200 copies of *"Apu and Me"*, and it sold out. I did not make a fortune, but it made up for the loss on Mrs Roberts' book.

I had time for small ambitions, too. One year I visited friends whose garden contained a wide expanse of well-manicured grass.

"How on earth do you mow it?" I asked. 'Do you have someone to do it?'

"We do it," came the reply, as they pointed to the ride-on mower in the garage.

"I have always wanted to sit on one of these and cut someone's grass!" I piped up. "It is one of my dreams." I approached the machine.

"Are you sure?" they asked in unison. A long lesson on how to drive the thing followed. It was heavy, and not easily manoeuvrable. I had a few runs on level ground, but when I drove across the slope, two wheels were on the down slope, and I struggled to stay upright. Then I realised I had to turn where the grass ended and the forest started. I chickened out. I stopped the engine, pushed the machine around, and returned to the house. I was left with much greater respect for people who use this contraption. It all looked so easy and effortless when others did it, but I am not sure I want to repeat my dream experience.

Another year, with the help of my nephew, Dani, I acquired an outboard motor for the rubber dinghy I have at my cool hide-out in Tahi, on a Danube island, called St Endre, or St Andrew's Island, which I inherited from my father, who bought it 40 years ago. I had extended and modernised the house, lifting the existing wooden structure, and building a new ground floor underneath it. Tahi is in a bit of a time warp. I love it for that, and for the fast flowing river, practically at the bottom of my garden, which I can now explore whenever I wish.

It is said that as one door closes another opens – that a death is often followed by birth. Within a year of Arzén's death, my first grandchild was born. I was over the moon. I was kept in the dark for a while about his name – Andrea teased me by giving me the clue that 'it is biblical', but they soon revealed that he was to be called Toby. I would have liked to be a young grandmother, but better late than never.

Fortunately, Toby's rather difficult birth – he was a very big baby – did not discourage Andrea, and a few years later a little brother to Toby was born on Christmas day and called, very appropriately, Robin. I believe we were all delighted, although Andrea had been hoping to be able to buy frilly clothes for a little girl. My grandsons have been a delight to me ever since. They come and visit me when they can, though the journey from the deep south of Kent to Manchester is uncomfortable, and they would like me to move closer to them. They have also invited me to holiday with them – a treat for us all.

So time drew on, and eventually, as I have said, I reached my seventieth birthday. I did not really know how I would celebrate this landmark, as I have friends in London and in the South and, of course, in and around Manchester – with over two hundred miles in between. Andrea solved the problem by suggesting I could have two birthdays, one in the South, and one in the North. I spent the first birthday at Andrea's house, and we invited a few old friends from London and Plymouth. In Manchester, my tennis club let me have the clubroom, and I invited my tennis friends, my musical friends, my writing friends, and those clients who had become friends to the celebration. In one corner of the club room I had a film of my recent Antarctic trip running, while Lily taught salsa to those willing to dance. It was not a boozy party, but I think we all enjoyed it. I woke up the following morning with the thought that I must have done something good in the past to be treated so well - and wondering how I should celebrate my eightieth birthday!